Moments
of
Truth

"Once again Joseph Nassal has taken the very ordinary aspects of life and opened them up so that we can see the extraordinary within. He plays with words like 'time,' cleverly turning phrases inside out. As he tells us of the people and events of his life, we are invited to look anew at our own, there to find both the seeds and the harvest of God's grace. All of this unfolds within the context of biblical faith. Or is it biblical faith that unfolds within the context of life? These reflections show us that it really makes no difference, they are all Moments of Truth."

—Dianne Bergant, CSA, Scripture Scholar,
Catholic Theological Union in Chicago

"If you want to know about grace, you could read the complex work of Karl Rahner — or you could take Moments of Truth *on retreat with you. With poetry, story and a succession of memorable images, Joe Nassal lays out everything we need to know about grace. I'd like to put this book into the hands of everyone I know who seeks a deeper spiritual life."*

—William Huebsch, author of a dozen books, including
A Spirituality of Wholeness: The New Look at Grace,
advisor to Benziger regarding whole community catechesis.

"What a great resource for the 'overbusies' on the spiritual path. In a culture that groans, 'I don't have time,' do yourself and those you love a big favor: Make time in your life for this book. Joe's writing challenged me to take a closer look at my warped obsession with time and made me ponder the consequences of what the Lord was saying to me through this wordsmith. If you buy this book for a friend, make sure to include a couple of highlighters. There are sentences in this book that you won't want to forget — and God doesn't want you to forget."

—Harold Ivan Smith, grief educator, author of
A Decembered Grief

MOMENTS
of
TRUTH

A Spirituality of Time, Grace and Sacred Space

Joseph Nassal

FOREST OF PEACE
Publishing
Suppliers for the Spiritual Pilgrim
Leavenworth, KS

Other Books by the Author:
(available from Forest of Peace Publishing)

Conspiracy of Compassion
Rest Stops for the Soul
Premeditated Mercy

Moments of Truth

copyright © 2002, by Joseph Nassal

Library of Congress Cataloging-in-Publication Data

Nassal, Joe, 1955-
    Moments of truth / Joseph Nassal.
        p. cm.
    ISBN 0-939516-58-6 (pbk.)
        1. Spiritual life—Catholic Church. I. Title.

    BX2350.3 .N37 2002
    242—dc21

                                                            2001056857

published by
Forest of Peace Publishing, Inc.
PO Box 269
Leavenworth, KS 66048-0269   USA
1-800-659-3227
www.forestofpeace.com

printed by
Hall Commercial Printing
Topeka, KS 66608-0007

1st printing: December 2001

Dedicated to

The Adorers of the Blood of Christ

for providing me with a sacred space
and more images of grace
than my heart could hold
during the three years
I lived on their holy ground
in Ruma, Illinois.

Acknowledgments

While this book is dedicated with gratitude to the Adorers of the Blood of Christ for providing the sacred space to write these reflections, I am especially grateful to Sisters Anastasia Rubenacker, Therese Anne Kiefer and Janet McCann who read the initial draft and offered valuable feedback. I am also deeply grateful to the priests, brothers and lay companions of my religious community for their witness, support and commitment to create safe places where truth can be spoken, heard and lived.

Family and friends have provided many moments of truth for me. The geography of grace afforded me the opportunity to live in close proximity to most of the family during the years I wrote this book and I am grateful for that time and those sacred connections. For most of the past thirty years I have not lived near family and so am grateful especially to my mom for her fidelity to the sacred art of letter writing. My sisters, Sharon and Mary, are also very good about keeping in touch via the more modern means of e-mail.

There is no better way to spend time than in the company of friends. For the past several years, I have traveled extensively with Tom Jacobs to give retreats. I am very grateful to Tom and his wife Beth for their friendship and faithful companionship on the journey. Tren Meyers, a friend for more than thirty years, continues to provide so many graced moments to delight my soul and lift my heart. My deepest thanks to Dianne Bergant, Bill Huebsch and Harold Ivan Smith for taking time from their busy schedules to review this material and offer their comments. They are prophetic and poetic teachers and tellers of the Truth.

Finally, to my friend and publisher, Tom Turkle, and Forest of Peace Publishing for providing such a hospitable place to express these reflections on time, grace and sacred space. And to Tom Skorupa, editor and friend, whose insights, suggestions and revisions, and the manner in which he makes them, can only be described as graceful.

Contents

Introduction **It's About Time:**
The Contemplation of Graced Time...9

Chapter One **Time Will Tell**:
Echoes of Grace and a Change of Pace...17

Chapter Two **The Nature of Grace**:
Experiencing the Pleasure and Pain of God...33

Chapter Three **States of Grace**:
Postcards from the Edge of Time and Space...50

Chapter Four **A Geography of Grace**:
Finding a Safe Place...62

Chapter Five **Vocation as Grace**:
Reflections on the One That Got Away...78

Chapter Six **Overshadowed by Grace**:
When Night Turns into Day...94

Chapter Seven **Saving Grace**:
When Time Goes By, Slowly...111

Chapter Eight **Time on Our Hands**:
Grace in Action...126

Chapter Nine **Signature of the Soul**:
Leaving Our Mark by Taking Care...147

Chapter Ten **Time To Go**:
The Grace of a Happy Death...163

Epilogue **The Day After**:
Finding Grace in the Ruins...176

The time has come for a decision and urgent commitment... a providential time [to be] met with a courageous and enlightened response.

—Thomas Merton

Introduction

It's About Time: The Contemplation of Graced Time

The contemplation of time
is the key to human life.
—Simone Weil

Timing Is Everything

Excuse me, do you have the time?

That's what this book is about, you know. It's about time. It's about how God is born in time and place. We call this reality "grace." Within the space of this book, we will attempt to articulate a spirituality of grace as it is present in the parameters of the times and places and people that comprise our lives.

Ever since writing a short story my sophomore year in high school that I gave the grandiose title *Time: The Essence of Life*, I have been fascinated with the concept of time. How little we have of it. How we try to save it. How we don't like to waste it. How we spend it but rarely can spare it. How there never seems to be enough of it and yet at times how we inflict violence upon it — we kill it.

It's about time.

Now that I've reached middle age, I'm amazed at how aerodynamic it is. Time seems to fly — at least, as they say, "when you're having fun." If that's true, then I must be having the time of my life now because time never moved so quickly. I can't seem to keep up with it.

When I was a child, time seemed to move slowly, at least during school days. But it picked up its pace on weekends. Snow days were supposed to slow time, but they never did, especially when friends came by to build forts or make angels and maybe even humans out of the snow.

Time is just as comfortable on land as it is in the air, especially when a deadline approaches and time is running out.

When we're nursing a wound, a well-meaning friend will often point out time's healing qualities.

But whether it's flying or running or healing, those of us who procrastinate believe in the promise that time is always on our side.

Like a beggar, time sits outside the gates of our every experience, longing for us to pay attention. Time says, "Hey, can you spare me?" Sadly, many of us are too busy, too often in a rush, even to notice the hands of time reaching out to slow us down. Time screams silently, "Take me with you! Take your time!" But time's cry is lost in the whirlwind of activity.

We pass time. It races to catch up with us until time passes. And then we wonder, where did time go?

It's about time.

Many of us look at time as an enemy or at least an opponent: We are up against the clock, in a race against time. But when we welcome time as a friend rather than an enemy, the presence of grace at the gates of our every experience helps us to get "under the clock."

I was in Kansas City recently and arranged to meet a friend for dinner. Since I had not yet been to the recently renovated Union Station, we decided to meet there. "I'll meet you under the clock," my friend said. There is a large clock hanging from the ceiling in the beautifully restored main atrium. My friend told me that when the trains were coming and going from Union Station, this was the place where people met: under the clock.

When friends meet under the clock rather than race against the clock, we slow the pace of this human race. In this meeting place under the clock, grace happens. In the realm of grace there is no need to ask, "What time is it?" because with a gentle, knowing smile, grace reminds us what someone once said: "In ancient cultures no one had a watch, but everyone had time. Now everyone has a watch, but no one has any time."

Do we have the time? Isn't it ironic that in an age of computers and cell phones, microwaves and fax machines, pay-at-the-pump gas stations that once were called "service stations" but are now "self-serve," and so many other modern conveniences designed to save us time, most of us still complain that we have so little time?

Graced Time and Space

Grace makes us aware of a fundamental fact: Even though we are members of the human *race* that we often perceive as a race against time, we are *human beings* first.

Grace sanctifies time and space, making that twin reality holy. Whenever a moment of grace occurs in our lives, it is a "holy hour" or a "sacred time." Living in this time, we become channels of God's grace to one another in all the places where we worship and work, pray or play, live and move and have our being. When grace comes down to earth, down to the ground of our being, we take off our shoes because we are standing on holy ground.

Christians believe that at a particular time and a specific place in human history, God came down to earth. God was born in time to sanctify and to redeem all creation and all creatures for all time. Because God came to earth, born in human time, grace is not a theological principle that is hard to grasp. Grace is not "out of this world" but rather is present right here, right now.

It makes one wonder: If God is everywhere, maybe we ought to walk through life in our bare feet.

For too long we have thought about grace by asking questions like, "How many angels can dance on the head of a pin?" In this book, we will see how grace is found in making angels in the snow with a friend.

Grace is tangible in time and space, something that can be seen and heard and held and smelled. We can see grace in the eyes of the beloved and the beauty of a sunset. We can hear grace in the laughter of children and listen for grace in the whisper of the dying or the deep sighs of the weary. We taste grace in a meal prepared by a friend or served in a soup kitchen. The aroma of grace arouses our sense of smell with fresh-cut flowers or fresh-baked bread. We hold grace in our hands when we catch another's tears, and wrap our arms around grace when we embrace a friend's fears or welcome the stranger to make herself at home.

These are moments of truth that reflect God's graced presence among us. These are the moments when God reveals to us our true identity, who we really are. We are children of God. We are God's Beloved. We don't have to pretend to be someone else or someone we are not. "We are the Beloved," Henri Nouwen wrote. "We are infinitely loved long before our parents, teachers, spouses, children and friends loved us or wounded us. That's the truth of our lives. That's the truth I want you to claim for yourself."

When we recognize and embrace our true identity, we will be faced in the course of our lives with moments of decision that call forth from us this truth of our lives. Thomas Merton wrote that these moments of truth reflect "the idea of *kairos* — the time of urgent and providential decision" and are "characteristic of Christianity, a religion of decisions in time and in history." But Merton wondered if we recognize these moments of truth when they come: "Is it possible that when the majority of Christians become aware that 'the time has come' for a decision and urgent commitment, the time has, in fact, already run out?" In this context, Merton pointed to Martin Luther King's sense of timing and noted how "providential time met with a courageous and enlightened response" and provided "the greatest example of Christian faith in action in the social history of the United States."

A Graced Odyssey Through Time and Space

The turn of the century and the beginning of a new millennium were seen by many as one of these "providential times." Many in the media made reference to Stanley Kubrick's film from the late 1960s, *2001: A Space Odyssey*. I would invite us to consider how our time on earth is a "grace odyssey" that invites us to come home to our truth about ourselves, our relationships and our God through the events and experiences of our lives. Through the lenses of time and place, we will see how this odyssey of grace is a spiritual adventure that reflects our agony and our ecstasy, our pain and our promise.

As you embark on this odyssey of grace, there are three items you need to take with you on the trip. First, you need a key. "The contemplation of time," Simone Weil wrote, "is the key to human life." As we contemplate time, how quickly it comes and goes, we shall see how time, like an open-face clock, holds in her hands the key to unlock our imaginations and find grace in all the experiences of our lives. In the divine imagination, God chose to travel through space and find a home on earth. In doing so, our God tells us we can find the divine presence anytime, anywhere. We can look to outer space and be struck with awe at the work of the creator of the universe; and we can look inside, to inner space, to see the presence of God's grace.

Second, you will need a mirror. If "timing is everything," then it is time to get in touch again with the truth that each of us is made in the image and likeness of God. We will never be able to recognize the face of God in others unless we first see the Divine One in ourselves. This is the pure and amazing thing about grace: It allows us to look in the mirror and see the face of God.

A third accessory for this grace odyssey is a compass. A few years ago when I was "out of sorts" — which means, I suppose, I was unable to sort through various options life presented — and feeling empty of grace, I went to see my spiritual director. After listening to me for almost an hour, Father Ed Hays reached into his pocket and gave me a small silver case. When I opened the lid, it was a compass. A compass can tell us which direction we're going — north, south, east, or west. But wherever we go, we start from where we are.

Wherever you are as you begin this book is a good place to be — so long as you know you are not alone, so long as you always carry with you an inner compass that points toward True Grace. With that inner compass in handf, I'll meet you under the clock where we will have the company of a lady named Grace.

A Lady Named Grace

Grace is her name.
Some may think she changed it
because they just don't call her
by name much anymore.

Grace sounds like an old-fashioned name,
like Sophia, her wise sister.
But Grace hasn't changed.
She is still pure gift.

She comes in various clothes
of different shapes and styles and sizes.
Though changing her appearance,
she still covers the world with love.

She wears white garments and a trace of perfume.
Sweet-smelling oil shimmers
on her forehead by the glow
of the candle she holds in her hand.

Her light burns away the darkness
and leaves a wholeness in our heart.
Her gentle hands touch blow-dried hair,
empowering us to become powerless.

Her tender, slender fingers
are adorned with rings
as the circle of her love
makes two bodies one.

Grace loves to celebrate.
She parties with thin wafers
of whole wheat that look more like cookies
than bread and life.

Grace drinks wine
and tells stories and pours out
her life as she whispers
words of healing and hope.

Grace says good-bye,
fare well,
with tears of joy as she accompanies
us on a journey beyond the sky.

Grace celebrates this birth to peace,
for this is the place
where grace received her name —
God.

Grace is the woman of water,
lady of light,
oil of gladness
in whom heaven embraces earth.

Grace is love —
pure, precious love.
Her scent of life dispels
the odor of decay and death.

She mingles with tears
and tingles with laughter.
Grace came to live
and to give life.

Her name is Grace,
but call her what you will,
save late —
she's always on time.

Some have tried to tie her up in dogmas,
imprison her in laws,
lose her in footnotes.
But you will always find her again.

Look for Grace in unlikely places
where people gather to celebrate life.
She will be standing naked before you
in innocence and beauty.

Grace will be wherever young and old
and in between
take time to love and laugh,
weep and mourn.

Grace will be present where people
remember and rejoice,
dance and dream and dare
to forgive.
There you will discover
the naked lady named Grace.
And you may recover or uncover
your soul.

Grace is her name,
but call her what you will.
She doesn't mind,
but she does care.

It is her nature
to care.
She is pure gift.
She is a face of God.

Chapter One

Time Will Tell:
Echoes of Grace and a Change of Pace

They wished and they murmured and whispered,
They said that to change was a crime.
Then a voice from nowhere answered,
"You must do what I say," said Time.
—Brian Patten, *The Tree and the Pool*

We begin this grace odyssey by recalling a lesson my mom tried to teach me when I was growing up and running late for school or racing out of the house to play ball with my friends. She used to say, "Take your time." She knew that if I was in such a rush to get to where I was going, I could easily fall along the way.

When I was younger, I would climb stairs two or three at a time. Now that I'm older and have a few scars from times I fell on my face, Mom's advice sounds wise: one step at a time.

In a world that places a high premium on speed, on this odyssey of grace we take one step at a time. Though we often find ourselves in a race against the clock, a race against time, I wonder if anyone really knows what time it is.

That is the question the musical group Chicago asked in a song in the late 1960s: "Does Anybody Know What Time It Is?" At the beginning of a new millennium, the question still lingers. But the question is an ancient one — as old at the book of Ecclesiastes, which provided the lyrics for another song from the 1960s that The Byrds turned into a hit, "Turn, Turn, Turn." The question is: "What time is it for you, for me, for us?"

Does anybody really know?

With the soul of a poet, the writer of the book of Ecclesiastes tries to answer the question, "What time is it?" by saying, "There is an appointed time for every affair under the heavens" (3: 1-8).

So in your life, in my life, is this a time to be born or a time to die?

Is it a time to plant or a time to uproot what we have planted?

Is it a time to kill or a time to heal?

We commit murder when we kill time. With our bare hands, we kill it. Robbery is also a common crime: We steal time, and then we wonder where it went. It was here just a minute ago. Where did time go? For most of us, work is the greatest thief of our time. It kidnaps the time we set aside to spend with family or friends and doesn't even leave a ransom note.

All these crimes against time are subtle but prevalent forms of the violence we do to ourselves. The language we use not only reflects our attitudes toward time; the way we speak reinforces those attitudes. For example, a few years ago I was running early one morning because I was running late. You see, I arrived at a suburban mall in Kansas City around 8:30 because I was in a hurry. I was driving to St. Louis to conduct a retreat that evening, but on the way I was going to stop and see my mom, who lives in the St. Louis area. Since it was her birthday, I wanted to get her a gift before hitting the road. What I didn't know is that most stores in most malls don't open until 9:30.

So I had an hour to kill. That is the violent metaphor I used. I thought about *killing* time instead of *spending* it. I fall into this language trap often. For example, when I was editor of a couple of magazines published by my religious community, I was confronted each month with *deadlines*. Why don't we think in terms of *lifelines*? After all, isn't that more accurate: Aren't we giving birth to something new, giving life to an article, a talk, a project, a plan?

What do you do when you have time on your hands? Do you kill it? If so, remember what Henry David Thoreau once wrote: "One cannot kill time without injuring eternity."

That phrase, "I'm just killing time," often finds its way into our conversation. But I wonder how our language would change if we recognized the presence of grace in every place where we have time on our hands? Sensing the presence of grace in the place where we're just sitting around or waiting for someone, we might say to one who asks if we're just killing time, "No, I'm healing time."

Is this a healing time for you? Or are you just killing time?

Does anybody really know what time it is? Do you know what time it is for you? Is this a time to tear down or a time to build? A time to weep or to laugh? A time to mourn or a time to dance?

In these time passages, we find one of the inherent dangers of being in relationship with others in community or in family life. When one of us wants to laugh and to dance, another might be in a period of weeping and mourning. When one of us is ready to build, another is in the process of tearing down. How rare it seems, even in our families, that our "heart watches" have the same time. Some of us clock watchers always seem to run five minutes fast so we won't be late for a very important date, while others are perpetually slow and always late. There is a priest in my community who is so well known for his tardiness that when we invite him to a meeting, we always tell him it starts at least one hour before it is actually scheduled to begin.

Some of us seem to exist on standard time, while others are on daylight savings time — trying to save as much daylight as possible. Is it because we're afraid of the dark?

Some of us live in different time zones, even though we reside under the same roof. Some of us are morning persons; others like to stay up late and are at our best after the sun has set. Some of us wake up the dawn, while others like to sleep late.

What time is it in your life, in my life, in our life?

Is it a time to gather stones or scatter them?

Is it a time to embrace or to keep our distance?

Is it a time to seek or a time to lose?

There are some of us who suggest there is no time to lose. Time is too precious to lose — we must try to save it. Others say that time is money and the clock is ticking. It is the loss of money, not time, that bends most people out of shape.

Those of us who have had a good time ask, "Where did the time go?" But for those having a bad time, the minutes struggle by and we wonder if this time in our life will ever end.

Is this a time to keep or a time to cast away?

Keeping time, having timekeepers, is important in sporting events. They don't keep score; they keep time. But they can't hold it for long. Each team is only given so many time-outs. And when a team uses all of its time-outs, time runs out.

What's the score in your game of life? Are you feeling like a winner, or do you always seem to be on the losing side? How many time outs have you taken? How many do you have left?

Some people tell us, "Don't worry about the time." But I wonder, "Does anybody really know what time it is?"

Is it a time to rend or a time to sew?

Is it a time to be silent or a time to speak?

Does anybody really know?

There is a time to love and a time to hate, the poet writes. There is a time for war and a time for peace.

Do we know what time it is?

What time is it for you?

From Cana to Calvary: How Time Flies

Jesus knew what time it was. Recall in John's Gospel (2: 1-11) when he's attending a wedding with his mother and a few of his disciples. At one point during the reception, his mother is concerned that the newlyweds will be embarrassed because the party is in full swing but the wine is in short supply. Mary tells Jesus, "They have no wine." Jesus responds to his mother's concern with what seems to be a rather cold remark: "Woman, what does that matter have to do with me? My hour has not yet come."

When Jesus refers to his "hour," he isn't looking at his watch. This is how most of us think of time: as a steady or straight line. The Greek word for this kind of time is *chronos*, from which we get the word "chronology." But in this scene from John's Gospel, Jesus is talking about *kairos* or the fullness of time.

The difference between *chronos* and *kairos* may be discerned in terms of how time flies. *Chronos* flies as a crow flies — in a straight line, from one event to the next, from point A to point B, from one experience to another. But *kairos* time is more like an eagle. It is majestic, circling high in the skies above us and nesting in cliffs where it finds rest. Eagles are graceful, noble creatures once thought — and in some cases and places this is still true — to be an endangered species.

Much like time itself.

Kairos time reflects a measure of time that ebbs and flows, rises and dies and rises again. It is in *kairos* time that we experience our moments of truth, and all these moments of truth are linked by grace. At the wedding feast at Cana when Jesus says, "My hour has not yet come," he connects his sense of timing with the cross. Cana and Calvary are intimately and intricately connected. This is clear in the way Jesus addresses his mother: "Woman." He doesn't say, "Mom, it's just not time yet." Nor does he address her with the more formal, "Mother, it's none of our business." Instead, he says, "Woman, my hour has not yet come." He calls her by this title again when his time has come, when his time is up. On the cross, he looks down and says, "Woman, behold your son!" And then to the beloved disciple he says, "Behold your mother!" (John 19: 26-27).

Jesus' reference to time and his "hour" that has not yet come invites soulful consideration. Has your time come? Are you still waiting for your hour? Or is it only — as Andy Warhol suggested — not an hour but only fifteen minutes?

That famous pop artist once said that everyone has his or her fifteen minutes of fame. The clock is ticking. According to Warhol, we've lost forty-five minutes. We only get fifteen. Have you had yours yet?

But fame — and acclaim — is not what Jesus is looking for at Cana. His hour is not about claiming a measure of fame or making a name for himself. It is about proclaiming salvation in his name. It is in the name of Jesus, Christians believe, that the world will be saved.

This is *kairos* time — not "saving time" but a time to be saved.

Jesus' Sense of Timing

Human though he was, Jesus had a divine sense of timing. In John's Gospel, Jesus often tells time. Remember how John's Gospel begins with the words, "In the beginning," and the last words Jesus says as he dies on the cross are, "It is finished." John links the events of Cana, where Jesus changed water into wine as his first sign to save a newlywed couple from embarrassment, with Calvary and his ultimate sign, where his death on the cross saved the world from sin. But throughout the Gospel there are references to time.

For example, the wedding at Cana occurred "on the third day" (2: 1). Jesus' encounter with Nicodemus happened "at night" (3: 1). As Jesus met the Samaritan woman at the well, "the hour was about noon" (4: 6). Jesus heals the son of the royal official, and "when he asked them at what time the boy had shown improvement, they told him, 'The fever left him yesterday afternoon about one.' It was at that very hour, the father realized, that Jesus had told him, 'Your son is going to live'" (4: 52-53).

After a long day of feeding the multitude with a few barley loaves and some dried fish, Jesus steals away to get some solitude "as evening drew on" (6: 16) only to have the disciples get caught in a storm at sea. By the time Jesus walks on the water toward them, "it was dark" (6: 17). The next day when the people who followed Jesus "found him on the other side of the lake, they said to him, 'Rabbi, when did you come here?'" (6: 25). But after he identifies himself as "the living bread come down from heaven" (6: 51), some of Jesus' followers are so disturbed that "from this time on, many of his disciples broke away and would not remain in his company any longer" (6: 66).

Still feeling the sting of this schism, Jesus decides not to go to Judea for the feast of booths because some of his opponents "were looking for a chance to kill him" (7: 1). Some of his disciples, however, think now is the time for Jesus to go public. "No one who wishes to be known publicly keeps his actions hidden" (7: 4), they argue. Jesus once again refers to timing: "It is not yet the right time for me, whereas the time is always right for you" (7: 6). Later in this same conversation as the disciples are anxious to attend the festival, Jesus tells them, "Go up yourselves to the festival. I am not going up...because the time is not yet ripe for me" (7: 8). When Jesus does finally go to the festival — and at various other points in John's Gospel — he escapes a close call "because his hour had not yet come" (7: 30).

The time of day is also important in John's Gospel. For example, it is daybreak when "he reappeared in the temple area" and the religious leaders bring him a woman caught in adultery. His opponents do this to trip him up, but Jesus neatly escapes their trap by saying, "Let the one among you who has no sin be the first to cast a stone at her." Then he bends down "a second time" to write on the ground (8: 7-9). Forgiveness is like the *dawn* that breaks through after a long night of guilt and shame, danger and deceit. After telling the woman, "Nor do I condemn you. You may go," Jesus tells his disciples, "I am the light of the world. No follower of mine shall ever walk in darkness; no, he or she shall possess the light of life" (8: 12).

The seasons of the year also contribute to understanding Jesus' sense of timing in John's Gospel. "It was winter, and the time came for the feast of the Dedication in Jerusalem" (8: 22). A cold front moves in as those opposed to Jesus' teaching become increasingly anxious to eliminate Jesus and lay him to rest in a cold stone tomb — the same place where Jesus' friend Lazarus has been "four days" before Jesus goes to pay his respects (11: 17). When Jesus tells them to "take away the stone," Martha objects, saying, "Lord, it has been four days now; surely there will be a stench" (11: 39). But when Lazarus comes shuffling out of that tomb, in the midst of this winter grief, there is a scent of springtime in the air.

But because of the euphoric uproar surrounding the resurrection of Lazarus, John says that "from that day onward there was a plan afoot to kill Jesus" (11: 53). This plan is put in action "six days before Passover" (12: 1), when Jesus returns to Bethany to celebrate Lazarus' new lease on life. At one point during the evening, "Mary brought a pound of costly perfume made from genuine aromatic nard, with which she anointed Jesus' feet" (12: 3). Judas gets his nose bent out of shape by the extravagance of using this costly perfume to soothe the rabbi's aching feet when the money could have been better spent on the poor. But Jesus defends Mary's timing by saying, "Leave her alone. Let her keep it against the day they prepare me for burial." Then, with the poignancy of a poet about to run out of time, Jesus predicts the plight of the poor for all time: "The poor you always have with you, but me you will not always have" (12: 7-8).

With another seasonal feast, the Passover, drawing near, Jesus tells his disciples, "The hour has come for the Chosen One to be glorified" (12: 23). He uses a seasonal image to describe his demise and rise: "I solemnly assure you, unless the grain of wheat falls to the earth and dies, it remains just a grain of wheat. But if it dies, it produces much fruit" (12: 24).

Familiar passages about time abound in John's account of the Last Supper, where Jesus offers his disciples a long discourse that amounts to his last will and "new" testament. "Before the feast of Passover, Jesus realizes that the hour has come for him to pass from this world to the Father" (13: 1), so he gets up from the table, kneels in front of his disciples and washes each one's feet. Later, the talk at the table turns to betrayal as Jesus announces that the one who would turn him in is in the room. Jesus identifies the betrayer to his beloved by saying it is "the one to whom I give the bit of food I dip in the dish" (13: 26). Notice how clear John is about the time of day when Judas eats the morsel of food and leaves the room: "It was night" (13: 30).

Timing is also an issue with the one Jesus had chosen to be "the rock" upon whom he would build his community of faithful disciples. At one point in the evening's conversation, Peter asks Jesus, "Lord, why can I not follow you now? I will lay down my life for you!" But Jesus tells Peter the precise time when he would deny even knowing him: "I tell you truly, the cock will not crow before you have three times disowned me!" (13: 37-38). The rooster calling forth the dawn would usher Peter into the darkest night of his life.

As he explains the fine print in his last will and new testament to his disciples on the night before his death, Jesus repeats a refrain that confuses his friends. "Within a short time you will lose sight of me, but soon after that you shall see me again" (16: 16). Jesus compares what they will feel after he departs from them to "a woman in labor" who "is sad that her time has come" but "when she has borne her child, she no longer remembers her pain for joy that a baby has been born into the world" (16: 21). Finally, after taking time to tell his disciples how much he loves them and that they are to "love one another," Jesus looks up to heaven and prays, "Father, the hour has come" (17: 1).

After his arrest, trial and sentence of death, Jesus is crucified. It is here on Calvary where the forces of love first displayed at Cana are fulfilled. "Seeing his mother there with the disciple whom he loved,

Jesus said to his mother, 'Woman, there is your son.' In turn he said to the disciple, 'There is your mother.' From that hour onward, the disciple took her into his care" (19: 26-27). Then, "realizing that everything was now finished," Jesus mentions his thirst, sips from the sponge soaked in sour wine pressed to his lips, and says, "It is finished" (19: 30).

When Time Runs Out

Yes, Jesus knew what time it was. The other Gospels also connect Jesus' sense of timing with the cross. In Luke's Gospel (9: 18-22), for example, there is a moment when he raises a question with his disciples about his identity. The time has come for Jesus to tell the disciples a secret. He doesn't ask them if they have the time, but rather asks, "Who do people say that I am?" In Luke's telling of this story, Jesus raises this important question as he comes out of solitude, out of seclusion, out of a time of quiet prayer. This question of identity must have been keeping time on Jesus' mind while he was praying. Now the time has come for the disciples to face the truth about Jesus.

It is Peter who faces the truth squarely. In response to Jesus' more pointed question, "Who do you say that I am?" it is Peter who says, "The Messiah of God" (9: 20). This could have been Peter's finest hour. His time has come to tell the truth. But with this profession of faith, Peter and the others are about to be ushered into a dark time, a time of suffering and grief. Jesus tells them to keep this a secret — it's not time yet. People will have to find this truth when they find the time.

And the truth is this: "The Chosen One must first endure many sufferings, be rejected by the elders, the high priests, and the scribes, and be put to death, and then be raised up on the third day" (9: 22).

Soon it would be night in the garden of Gethsemane: a time to weep and to mourn. Soon after that it would be high noon on the hill of Calvary: a time to die. And seventy-two hours after that — for those watching the clock instead of the calendar — it would be dawn at the tomb: a time to be born. Again. A time to laugh and a time to dance.

So, what time is it for you, for me, for us? Does anybody really know? Whatever time it is for you, trust that God knows what time it is. It's simple enough, really.

The time is now. Here's a story about a young man that reflects how "time will tell" if we only listen. What time tries to tell us is how we use it, how we spend it, how we don't like to waste it, how we never have enough of it, and what happens when we try to steal it.

The call came around four o'clock on a Thursday afternoon. Bill was in law school and had a big test in Contract Law on Friday morning. He was chained to his desk, where he was most of the time. You see, Bill's parents, and especially his mother, always wanted him to be a lawyer. His father was a lawyer; so was his grandfather. The study and practice of law ran in his family's bloodstream. From his earliest recollection, Bill never considered any other profession. He would be a lawyer.

"Bill, you have a phone call," a voice screamed from the hallway.

"Tell whoever it is to call back. I'm busy," Bill shouted back.

"It's your sister. She's calling long distance. Sounds important."

Long distance or not, Bill was upset. He had too much studying to do to talk to his sister just now. His agitation was evident in his voice as he answered the phone.

"Bill," his sister said softly, "it's Mom. She's had a stroke."

The words hit Bill like a thunderbolt. "How bad is she?"

"Billy, get home as soon as you can," his sister said. And Bill told her he would be on the next bus.

But when he got back to his room and saw all the books and materials open for his big test the next morning, Bill stopped. He knew the test accounted for most of his grade in Contract Law. He was ready for the test and didn't want to miss it or ask for an extension. Even though he heard the urgency in his sister's voice, somewhere inside he could sense his mother was going to be all right. He would stay the night, study as much as he could, take the test and fly home the next day instead of taking the bus. Yes, that's what he would do. Besides, he was sure his mother would be okay. She would want him to stay and take the test. Maybe he was rationalizing, but rationalization is a first cousin of procrastination.

He called his sister, told her that he would be home the next morning and asked her to pick him up at the airport. Before he hung up the phone, he asked if there had been any change in their mother's condition. "She's holding her own," his sister told him.

The next morning, Bill took the test. As he rode to the airport, he felt good. He thought he had aced the exam. His mother would be proud. But then, as he sat on the plane, the seriousness in his sister's voice the day before echoed again: "Get home as soon as you can."

When he got off the plane, his sister was there to meet him. When he saw her, he knew his time had run out. He was too late. "Mom died about 9:00 this morning," she said. His mother died at the exact hour he started the test in Contract Law.

When Bill arrived home, the family gathered in the kitchen. Bill's father brought to the table four letters, one addressed to each of the four children. Bill looked at the envelope with his name etched in his mother's familiar handwriting.

Bill read his letter slowly.

My dearest Billy,

I have just finished reading a wonderful book called In a Chinese Garden. *It's about a doctor named Frederick Loomis, a well-respected obstetrician, who for years brought new life into the world. The book tells of the many valuable lessons he learned as he spent all his time and energy on his patients. But near the end of his career, he realized he had not spent much time and energy on his own life. Then one day he received a letter from Peking, China, that changed all that. It was from a young woman who at one time was a patient at the hospital where Dr. Loomis worked. She had been pregnant and lost her baby. This young woman's name was also Loomis, so when the doctor learned that she had lost her baby, even though she wasn't his patient, he asked the nurses about her and went to see her. The young woman wrote to thank Dr. Loomis for his visit many years before. He had not said much, but she would always remember how he sat at her bedside, touched her arm and spoke in a very comforting voice. She remembered how his face seemed so kind and yet so very tired. When Dr. Loomis left the room, she asked one of the nurses about this doctor, and the nurses told her that he was at the hospital all hours of the day and night.*

Then she came to the purpose of writing to Dr. Loomis so many years later — and my purpose in writing to you, my dearest son. This woman was staying at a private home in Peking and had gone out into the garden that afternoon. On the garden wall she noticed a bronze plaque on which was inscribed in Chinese these simple words: 'Enjoy yourself. It's later than you think.' She wrote to Dr. Loomis how those words had changed her life. Though still grieving the loss of her baby, those words gave her courage to once again enjoy life and make every moment count for something, for someone. She concluded her letter by writing that she wanted to pass on that simple message she found in the garden to Dr. Loomis, hoping that maybe he would reflect on his own busy ways.

That night Dr. Loomis couldn't sleep. He couldn't let go of the message on the garden wall, 'Enjoy yourself. It's later than you think.' The next morning, Dr. Loomis went into his office and announced to his staff that he was taking a vacation. He went to a resort in South America where he stayed for three months, relaxing, rejuvenating himself, and leaving all his cares behind.

Sometimes we all get so busy that we forget to tell each other how much we love each other. We take our love for granted. But I know how much you love me, Billy, and I hope you know how much I love you and always will. Know that I'm so proud of you, Billy. You will be a great lawyer — great in whatever walk of life you feel called, but remember you are great right now. You are my beloved. I love you, Billy. So, since the Bible teaches us that none of us know what time it is — none of us knows the day or the hour we will be called home — take your time and enjoy your life.

Love,

Mom

The Dividing Line

This is the dividing line time draws at the gates of our experience. It is the dividing line between regret and remembrance. The dividing line that can be summed up in five words, "I did not have time."

This is the line drawn in the sand that divides the wise from the foolish. Like sand through an hourglass, we only have so much time. Fools rush in because they believe they have all the time in the world. Wise ones tend to spend time in ways that focus their attention on this present moment. That's why the wise see the sand slipping through the hourglass and sense how the soul needs to walk on the beach every now and then in the company of a friend. They know that time is on their side not because they procrastinate but because they are mindful of what they are doing, whom they are with and who they are — most of the time.

Time is all we have. Remember my mom's advice: Take your time. Remember Bill's mom's message, written on the Chinese garden wall: "Enjoy your life. It's later than you think."

On the divine calendar, a thousand years are like a day. No wonder God never feels the need to punch a clock. God can afford some leisure. The creation story indicates that God took a day off after a creative six-day workweek. God knows the need for Sabbath time; do we?

Sadly, many in our world don't know what time is trying to tell them because they don't take time to listen. They are in a hurry to get where they are going. One such person was Barry, a businessman in his early thirties with a bright and promising future. He had a nice home, a good marriage and two small children he adored. However, to provide for his family in the way he wanted and to rise even higher in the estimation of his superiors, Barry worked extremely long hours. In the course of a twenty-four hour day, something had to give. And the push and pull of time on Barry's life pulled mainly in the direction of work. He always seemed to be on the run, going from a business luncheon to a board meeting downtown and then hurrying back to his office. On the way, he often "saved" time by calling his wife on his car phone and telling her he would be working late.

One day Barry was on his way to an important meeting with a top client. As usual, he was running late. Since punctuality is one of those keys on the ring called success, he was driving faster than he should have been. He was going by a playground and didn't notice the school, let alone the sign: *Slow — Children Playing*. Suddenly a ball, followed closely by a little girl, flashed in front of his car. The rest was a blur to Barry, except for the terrified look on the little girl's face. That look would be etched on his mind for a long time.

Barry slammed on the brakes, jumped the curb and crashed into a tree. The screeching tires and thunderous crunch brought people out of their homes to see what had happened. What they saw in the middle of the street was Barry, weeping and holding a shaken but unharmed little girl in his arms.

As Barry cradled the little girl as if she were his own, he understood something about priorities. So what if he was late for the meeting or lost an account because he was tardy? So what if he didn't finish all his work today? It could wait. What couldn't wait were his little girls. That night he was home to tuck them in bed.

That sign we see near school playgrounds may provide an insight and a challenge to cultivating a prayerful, soulful, graceful life: *Slow — Children Playing.* True prayer combines a sense of paying attention with an attitude of awe. In prayer, we focus our attention on God but are engaged with a sense of amazement. It's very much like a child who sees something for the very first time and is hypnotized or entranced by it. The child is able to concentrate on the object totally and yet is full of wonder about it.

Maybe that's why Jesus told his disciples that we must become like little children to inherit the kingdom of God (Mark 10: 15). When we pray, we seek to have the attitude of a child and to see the world in all its wonder as if for the very first time.

If we really want to know what time it is, this may become our mantra: *Slow — Children Praying.*

Or, we might listen to what time will tell us.

I can hear time saying, "Hold on a second."

Or, "Wait a minute."

This is what we say when someone is in a hurry. The other person is ready to go, but we're not ready yet. So we say, "Wait a minute," or, "Hold on a second." But minutes and seconds slip through our fingers like sand through an hourglass. Yet unlike that sand, minutes and seconds don't leave a trace.

Grasping at straws is easier than holding on to seconds. They are so slippery. They slip through our fingers, out of sight and out of mind.

Robert Louis Stevenson once observed that "quiet minds cannot be perplexed or frightened, but go on in fortune or misfortune at their own private pace, like a clock during a thunderstorm." I like that image. Of course, Stevenson wrote before the age of electricity. Now many of our clocks are plugged in, and at some time during a thunderstorm the electricity usually goes off. When the power is off, the clock stops. When the power returns, the clock starts from scratch, blinking 12:00, and continuing from there as if to say this zero hour is correction time, blinking so you know the clock must be reset.

When the power goes off, when we're stuck or perplexed or frightened, we are like the clock that goes back to the stroke of midnight and blinks all day. It's time to reset our relationship to time and grace.

But a clock that runs on batteries keeps time during a crisis. So long as the batteries are fresh we will always know what time it is. When our batteries are charged by times of prayer, we become peaceful of mind, quiet of heart, and we can ride out any storm.

At the beginning of this chapter I mentioned some of the crimes, like murder and theft, that we commit against time. But perhaps the greatest criminal act we commit against time is our failure to listen to what time has to tell us. We think we have all the time in the world, and yet none of us knows how much time we have left.

So with all these crimes being committed against time, here's the best advice I know to stop the crime wave: go fishing. "Time is but a stream I go a-fishing in," wrote Thoreau in *Walden*. "I drink at it; but while I drink I see the sandy bottom and detect how shallow it is. Its thin current slides away, but eternity remains."

We must do what time tells us.

In the end, this is what time says: Slow down. Take one step at a time. Taking our time doesn't help us get where we are going any sooner, but when we take life "one step at a time" we will begin to sense the presence of God in between the steps.

This is where life finds meaning: in between the steps of our busy lives.

Taking our time will not slow down the hands of time. The hands of time move in a motion all their own. But this is where we find our own truth: in the spaces between the hands of time. It is in these sacred spaces when we recognize the grace of God that we perceive our moments of truth and are reminded that time is on our side.

Prayer for Time Keepers
and Clock Watchers

Blessed are you, God of all creation,
for you have given to us your gracious gift of time.
In your infinite wisdom, you teach us how to take time,
not for granted, but to spend it wisely and well
in the company of those whose faces glow
with the radiance of your redemption.

We learn how precious is your gift of time, O God,
when we look at our hands.
The time lines drawn there remind us
how foolish we are when we pick up the pace
and race in endless pursuits that leave us
always running behind or out of time.

Or how we often kill your gift of time
with instruments of destruction —
boredom, worry, resentment and fear.
O God of Wisdom, you invite us to open our hands
to see we are living on your clock,
under your timeless watch.

Your time is always borrowed time.
But borrowed time is blessed time
because it keeps us prepared.
We don't take each other for granted.
We don't take to telling lies
because when we live on borrowed time
we only have time for the truth.

When we live in your time zone, O God,
we can waste time and see this waste
not as refuse to be thrown away
but as refuge, time well spent
in the sanctuary of our own or another's soul,
time to be recycled again and again
for all time.

Chapter Two

The Nature of Grace: Experiencing the Pleasure and Pain of God

The butterfly counts not months but moments,
And has time enough.
—Tagore

One dwells with God by being faithful to one's nature.
One crosses God by trying to be something one is not.
—Parker Palmer

It is the nature of grace to hang out at that stream where time goes fishing. Grace is at the beginning of the journey and at the finish line. Grace is at all those lifelines drawn on the landscape of our lives by the hands of time that remind us that the time is now. Like time, grace doesn't take sides but is always on our side. In our efforts to save time, grace saves us. It's the nature of grace to save. Here's a parable to illustrate the connection between the nature of grace and our concept of time.

Brad told his wife Karen that he would be "back in a minute." It was a Saturday, and Brad was going to clean up the garage. But before he started what he imagined would be an all-day project, he wanted to run a few errands. Besides, his two children were still in bed, and the night before they promised to help their dad clean out the garage. But it was too early to wake them — it was Saturday, after all — so he would let them sleep in. Besides, he would be back in a minute.

When the children came downstairs for breakfast, rubbing the sleep from their eyes, Brad had already been gone for more than an hour. The children asked their mother, "Where's Dad? He's not working in the garage already, is he?" Karen told them he had a few errands to run and would be "back in a minute."

When Brad did not return after a couple of hours, Karen started to worry. She kept looking at the clock and making excuses when the children would come into the kitchen from watching cartoons and ask if their dad had come back yet. "He probably stopped at the flea market," she told them. "You know your father, he can never pass up a bargain." That was why the garage needed cleaning out in the first place. Brad was famous for stopping by flea markets and garage sales and buying other people's junk to store in his own garage. Then he'd forget about it, and once a year he had to clean out his own garage and arrange for a sale of his own.

Karen tried to keep busy cleaning the house, but when Brad's "back in a minute" had stretched to more than four hours, she was very worried. She told the children to go to the garage and get a head start, hoping Brad would be back any minute. "Your dad will be so proud of you to see you working when he gets home."

The children had been working only fifteen minutes when their dad pulled up in the driveway. The station wagon was loaded with stuff he had picked up at the flea market. When Brad saw the children, he gave them a hug and said, "I'm sorry, guys, I lost all track of time. Your mom is probably worried sick. I told her I'd be back in a minute."

When Karen saw her husband walk in the house, she breathed a sigh of relief that he was all right, threw her arms around him and kissed him. Then, she whispered in his hear, "Now that I know you're not dead, I'm going to kill you for not calling!"

When a person tells us, "I'll be back in a minute" but doesn't return for a few hours, we get worried. It is the nature of grace not only to be present at the beginning of life and at the end of life but in all those in-between times of our lives when we worry and wonder if everything is all right. Grace allows us to trace the lines of God's love in our own faces and the faces of one another. In both the "worry" lines that cause wrinkles and the lines caused by smiles and laughter that make us look forever young, grace gives us a glimpse of the face of God.

The challenge that grace presents is to keep the house of our hearts in order because we never know when God will show the divine face. It would be ideal, of course, if God would call first with the precise hour of his arrival so we could tidy up the house and be ready when God comes. Like Karen, who was worried sick when Brad wasn't "back in a minute," if God would only let us in on the cosmic calendar, let us take a peek at the divine date book, we wouldn't have to worry so much. But God doesn't punch a clock. The divine instruments for telling time are not like our own. God doesn't go by the clock or the calendar. We are the ones who put God on the clock, try to fit God in our time frames, and work God into our busy schedules.

But the nature of grace suggests that we ultimately live by God's time. Remember in Matthew's Gospel when Jesus told his disciples the parable about the wise and foolish bridesmaids (25: 1-13). The moral of the story is "keep your eyes open, for you know not the day or the hour." It is the nature of grace to keep us prepared. There is no time or term limit mentioned; the only admonition is to watchfulness. "Keep awake," Matthew advises, "for you do not know on what day your Lord is coming" (24: 42).

It is the nature of grace to save, but no matter how hard we try, we cannot save time. If, however, we spend each day giving praise to God when the sun comes up and every night giving thanks to God for the graces of the day, we will be ready whenever our time comes.

By the way, you may wonder why in this age of cell phones Brad didn't call his wife Karen to tell her he'd be late. Well, what he told the children was true — he did lose track of time. You see, at the flea market he ran into his old college roommate and they went out to breakfast and rode around the city for a couple of hours going over old times. Brad invited him over to the house, but he couldn't make it because he was busy that afternoon. So Brad invited him for supper that Saturday night.

And because Karen had cleaned the house so thoroughly that morning to take her mind off Brad not being "back in a minute," the house was sparkling clean for their guest that night. After Brad and the children worked several hours that afternoon, the garage was cleaned out too. And once all the junk was set out on the curb for the sanitation department to pick up, Brad said to the children, "Now, let's unload the back of the car and put away all the great stuff I picked up this morning."

Naming Grace

The nature of grace evokes an intimacy with God that speaks of recognizing the face of God in the faces of all we know and love. It reflects a sense of gratitude for each moment we spend in the company of family and friends, and relishing those times of surprise when someone from our past shows up to renew and refresh "old times." We name these times as "graced moments," and though we call these people who are most important to us by different names, they all share a common name: Grace.

I met Sister Mary Grace when I gave a retreat in Ruma, Illinois, in 1992. She was 90 and had been a religious for 60 years. Though math is not my strong point, I did some quick subtraction and said, "You were 30 when you came to the convent. That was kind of late in those days." Grace told me she had been a switchboard operator and went by the name "Fanny." Her eyes grew wider behind her coke-bottle-like glasses as she said, "Father, I was engaged to be married, but he dumped me! But I was so happy because I'd always wanted to be a nun!"

For 60 years of religious life, Grace was a housekeeper. She took care of the other sisters on mission so they could take care of the students they taught in school. She went from convent to convent during those 60 years and always took the lowest place. At the time I met her, Sister Mary Grace was still folding laundry at the convent.

My impression of Grace was of a woman who humbly accepted God's call in her life, her soul saturated with sacred simplicity. To meet Grace was to meet a person on whom God's spirit rests. Sister Mary Grace knew that she was blessed by God, that she was God's beloved.

Behind those thick glasses that magnified the eyes of Sister Mary Grace, I saw the light that can only come when we embrace the graced reality that we are loved by God. Though her eyesight was fading, her insight was forever young. I could see in her smile that this woman knew that God was very fond of her. I could sense in the words she spoke and the witness she lived that she knew she was God's beloved. It seems the challenge for each of us who has been given the name *Christian* is to spend our lives *living down* and not *up* to that name. For, you see, being Christian begins and ends on our knees, serving the rest.

When Sister Mary Grace died, I could see her taking the lowest place in heaven and God saying to her, "No, Grace, come higher. You belong here by my side. For you knew, throughout your 90 years of life, that it was I who held your hand. Take my hand, now, you who spent your life taking the lowest place, come and stay forever by my side."

The Second Nature of Grace

Our vocation in life has been knitted together by the gracious and graceful hands of God. The hands of the Divine One stretch across time and space to grasp our own hands, leading us out of darkness and isolation and fear into the light of God's love. Because Sister Mary Grace was so aware of her intimate relationship with God, she carried out her vocation with great dignity and sacred simplicity. She was self-aware but not self-conscious. When we are self-conscious, we worry too much about how we look, about what will happen if we make a mistake, about what others see or are saying about us.

Sister Mary Grace was self-aware — she was conscious of God's love for her. She knew who she was and did not try to be someone she was not. This self-awareness allowed her to live in such a way that she knew it was God's grace that guided her every step, wrote her every word, underscored her every act. Living in this way became second nature to Sister Mary Grace. She didn't have to think about it. She had nothing to hide. She simply lived as one loved by God. She knew it and didn't have to prove it.

This is the "second nature" of grace: The knowledge of God's love for us is so imbedded in our bones that we don't have to think about it. God's love and the identity that comes from this love are second nature to us. Unfortunately, most of us spend our lives trying to prove our love for God because we can't quite believe that God loves us unconditionally. When we do this, when we live out of fear of making a mistake and losing God's love, then we are never quite able to embrace this second nature of grace.

For Christians, the first instance of what in time may develop into grace's second nature comes in baptism. The grace of baptism is that our lives are claimed for God in a very unique and intimate way. In baptism, we are given the name Christian. It is a name that colors with the love of Christ all that we are and all that we do. In baptism, we are grasped by the hand of God and given a new lease on life.

Claimed for God, named for Christ, we are to be a spirit-filled people who live as God's beloved. This is our true identity. This is the very nature of our relationship with God: We are God's beloved. Inspired by God's grace, we live as did the one for whom we are named. The incarnation of Jesus means that God's grace is born in space and time: God has become one with us. Throughout his life on earth, Jesus tried to reflect how intimately this grace is connected to us. From his baptism by John in the Jordan until his death on the cross, Jesus' mission was about revealing the nature of grace — the presence of God — in each and every experience of our lives.

Until it becomes second nature to us.

The Pleasure of God

It is the nature of grace to explore the caves of our soul or climb the heights of a mountain where we come face to face with our expectations. But instead of writing a report about what we find in the depths or keeping minutes of our meeting with God on the mountain, we spend the minutes or hours or days in God's presence just for the pleasure of it all.

In these quiet moments alone with God at the kitchen table or on the back porch, in the corner of our room in front of our prayer shrine or on a long walk in the grove in the early morning hours, our souls are nourished. We breathe in the fresh air of God's gracious love for us even as we thank God for the gift of life. In these moments of grace, we ask only that our lives be pleasing to God by giving us the courage to be true to the gifts God has given to us and to be true to ourselves. When we use our God-given gifts in the service of others and in the pursuit of God's dream for us and for the world, we will experience the "pleasure of God."

That phrase comes from the film *Chariots of Fire*, in which there is a scene that captures well what it means to live a grace-filled life. A devout Christian from Scotland is one of the fastest human beings on earth. His family is scheduled to leave for a missionary trip to China, but this young man is in training for the Olympics. He is torn between his passion for running and a need to fulfill the requirements of his religious belief. When his sister confronts him because he has decided to follow his dream of running in the Olympics rather than going with the family on their missionary tour, he tells her he remains devout and faithful. But then he says to her, "When I run, I feel the pleasure of God."

This is one of the best ways I know to express the nature of grace. When we use our gifts to give glory to God, we will feel the pleasure of God. Or to paraphrase Joseph Campbell, if we find our bliss we never have to work a day in our lives.

There is a difference, isn't there, between creating something for pleasure and making something for profit? If we create a work of art or write a poem or play an instrument or sing a song, we are called "professional" if we are paid for it. But are we passionate? When the two come together, we call it grace. But if we create something only to make money or to have it be useful but not necessarily meaningful, then it loses some of its glow.

One of the great temptations in life is to live up to other peoples' expectations rather than embrace our own gifts. How difficult it is to take to heart Polonius' advice to Laertes in *Hamlet*: "This above all: to thine own self be true." Finding that true self is not easy, but the risks of not doing so are huge because as Parker Palmer writes, "One crosses God by trying to be something one is not." But in those moments of truth when we are true to ourselves, when we embrace our talents and our limits, we experience an inner peace, an inward calm, which no outside forces can shake because we know who we are.

But beware: When we enter into silence and solitude to discern our true nature and vocation in life, we give our demons a chance to speak and our shadows a chance to dance. We can become self-conscious rather than self-aware. When we are self-conscious, we are afraid of what others might think or afraid we don't quite measure up to God's pleasure. These are times when our hope collapses and then rises again.

This is the place where God's wisdom meets our fear.

When Wisdom Meets Fear

We'll call fear *Phil* and wisdom *Sophia*. We begin the story with Phil sitting in the darkness of a deserted street. A voice inside his mind screams, "Phil, you worthless, lazy lout! Why don't you get a job? Aren't you tired of hanging around these dark alleys, begging for nickels and feeling sorry for yourself? Get a life, man!"

Phil had a life once. He had a job too. He was an investment banker. But he got scared. Handling other peoples' money became too much for him. Maybe it was the savings and loan scandal a few years before that made him nervous. It twisted Phil into knots. Finally, he could no longer do the work he was trained to do. When his performance level dropped dramatically, he was fired.

Being unemployed created tensions at home. His wife left him. His friends abandoned him. Phil lost his house, his family and his circle of support. He was alone. Once he sat in a bright office with his hands busy at the computer or punching numbers on the phone as he called clients; now he sat in darkness and used his hands to hold up his head.

Phil considered himself a failure. He thought his boss was right to fire him. And he would never forget those words his boss shouted at him that day — the words that continued to ring in his ears: "You worthless, lazy lout."

What had gone wrong? He had so much promise. Oh, maybe not as much as some of his colleagues in the company — the ones who were given the larger accounts. But still he was given his share of wealthy clients. Why had he wasted his talent? Why had he buried it beneath the fear that rose up inside him? He knew it was fear that got the best of him and ultimately destroyed his career. He knew it was fear that left him here in the darkness.

"Excuse me?" a voice from the darkness said. "Could you tell me where Independence Avenue is?

Phil should have been startled by this voice, but he wasn't. He kept his hands on his head, shaking his head slowly.

There was silence for a moment. Then someone came closer. Phil could feel another's breath upon his face. He looked up and saw the face of an old woman, her wrinkled skin now dimly illuminated by the orange and red lights of a nearby neon sign. "May I help you?" she whispered.

Phil looked into her eyes. She had just asked him for help, and once again he proved himself worthless. Now she wanted to help him. Maybe give him some loose change out of her purse. But she didn't open her purse. Instead, she touched his arm. "My name," she said, "is Sophia. Is there anything I can do for you?"

"You can leave me alone," Phil said as he brushed her arm away.

But Sophia stayed. She sat down next to Phil on the step and pulled her coat collar up around her neck. "Kind of cold out tonight," she said.

Phil covered his ears with his hands, but not because of the cold.

They sat in silence on that step for awhile. The darkness closed in around them. Finally, Phil broke the silence. "Listen, lady, can't you see I want to be alone?"

"Yes," she said. "I can see that."

"Then why don't you just go?"

"Because I don't know where Independence Avenue is, and I thought you could help me."

"I already told you I didn't know. Now beat it."

But still Sophia stayed. "That's okay," the old woman said. "I'll find it."

Sophia: The Naked Truth

Like her sister, Grace, Sophia is another name for God. God is a generous grandmother who extends her hands to those in need. We find her reaching out her hands to the poor and extending her arms to the needy. It is said that Sophia built herself a house that she keeps with simplicity and grace, reflecting her inner harmony. But Sophia also walks the streets to reach out to those who sit in darkness and fear.

Wisdom is woven into the fabric of her life because she knows who she is. She realizes that beauty fades and charm can be deceiving, so she lives with integrity and justice. Sophia labors with love, a love she deposits in the hearts of those she touches in the routine of her day. She sees the love she deposits drawing interest. The dividends compound daily and are paid out at a rate that reflects unlimited possibilities. Small acts of compassion, simple gestures of kindness, exchanges of divine glances and sacred moments of beauty — all these are seen not as expenses but as investments. They're an inheritance, if you will, from a God, who, like a gracious grandma, invests grace in each of us freely and desires only that we use her gifts by spending our time, our talent and our treasure to benefit others.

The offspring Sophia produces are not afraid of the dark because they know the darkness of evil or shame or blame cannot seep so deep as to destroy their soul. These children know that only one thing can destroy the soul, and that is fear.

This is what caused Phil to bury his inheritance. He was afraid: afraid of his boss, afraid of himself, afraid of winning, afraid of losing, afraid of the dark. That is precisely where his fear led him: thrown out into the darkness.

Courage and fear are not opposite emotions. A cowardly spirit seems contrary to a courageous one, but both know fear well. A coward is one who allows fear to gain the upper hand. A hero knows and understands fear. But the person of courage will not allow fear to be the determining factor when the moment of truth arrives.

In *The Road Less Traveled*, Scott Peck says that "most people think courage is the absence of fear. The absence of fear is not courage; the absence of fear is some kind of brain damage. Courage is the capacity to go ahead in spite of the fear or in spite of the pain. When you do that, you will find that overcoming fear only makes you stronger."

When our moment of truth arrives, when our hour has come, we may have more than a measure of fear. But if we give into our fear, the hands of time will pass us by, and we will miss our finest hour. There are many moments when such truth arrives in our lives. These are the moments when truth is spoken without regret or revision. It is the unvarnished truth. The bare facts. The naked truth. Most of the time we dress truth up to make it presentable. But truth is never self-conscious.

At least the true self is not self-conscious. The false self is always worried about what others think. When the moment of truth arrives, the false self will worry: How am I dressed? Is my hair okay? Is my tie straight? Do I have ketchup on my shirt? Do I look okay?

Fear is the absence of hope. When we are afraid, we do not use our Grandma God's gifts in the service of others. We keep them to ourselves and bury them in unmarked graves.

There is a Chinese saying: "When the archer shoots for no particular prize, he has all his skills. However, when he shoots to win a brass buckle, he is already nervous. And when he shoots for a gold prize, he sees two targets, he goes blind, and is out of his mind."

Like the archer, Phil's skill or gifts had not changed, but the thought of winning a prize began to divide him. He began thinking more of winning than of shooting. The need to win and the consequent fear of losing began to drain him of his power, of his gift, of his ability. After a while, he began to lose his power to believe in himself. The pressure to win, to outdistance his colleagues, to earn more money, began to gnaw on his nerves. He didn't possess the talent some of his colleagues did, and he possessed more than others, but the pressure to perform, to excel, was always a constant.

Rather than embracing his own gifts, his own level of competence, he began to compare his gifts with others. Then the fear of losing began to get the best of him — the fear of not being able to keep up with the others, the fear of not being able to live up to his abilities. The fear of making a mistake. And because he was afraid of making a mistake, he started taking fewer risks.

Fear had robbed him of his memory. He forgot that the number of gifts, the amount of ability, is not important. All of us have been given different gifts and to varying degrees. The point is not how many gifts or talents we've been given but how we invest those gifts in building a more just society and a peaceful world.

And our abilities do not determine our reward. So long as we invest these gifts wisely, we shall know the same reward: "the pleasure of God." As Teilhard de Chardin said, "Joy is the most infallible sign of the presence of God." Joy, the pleasure of God, is what Phil sensed from this wise old woman sitting by his side on that step. He sensed in her a spirit of joy. She was not afraid. Her house was in order. Her heart was in order. She was not afraid. Yes, Phil could see it now in the wrinkles of her face as she smiled. He could see it in her eyes illuminated by that neon sign. There was joy in this woman.

"Do you see it now?" Sophia says. "The opposite of joy is not sadness. The opposite of joy is fear. Like a thief in the night, fear lingers in the shadows waiting for the opportunity to lure us into the darkness where joy is mugged, robbed and left for dead."

There is only one fear worth having, Sophia says. "Happy are those who fear God." At first glance, joy and fear seem to be an odd couple, a marriage of opposites. But upon reflection, it is a marriage made in heaven. That's because fear of God is a healthy fear, not a helpless fear. It is a fear we teach our children when we say: Be sure to look both ways before crossing the street. It's a fear that reminds us we are not walking our own way, but God's way. It's a way marked out for us from the beginning of time when our Grandma God said, "Here, O child of light, here are your gifts. Use them wisely and well. And remember, they are freely given to you."

And so the work of creation continues. The gifts we have are to be used in the service of others. In serving others, we serve God. In looking into the face of another whom we have served, we see true joy. We see the face of God.

"I must be going now," Sophia whispers in Phil's ear. "You take care of yourself. It's cold out tonight."

As she gets up to leave, Phil touches her arm. "Wait," he says. "It's not right for you to be walking these streets so late at night."

Sophia smiles and says, "I'm not afraid."

For the first time, Phil smiles, and says, "But I am. May I walk with you awhile?"

As they walk down the sidewalk, arm and arm, Phil asks, "What was that street you were looking for again?"

"Independence Avenue," Sophia says. "Do you know where it is?"

"Not exactly," Phil says. "But I think we're heading in the right direction."

Grace Under Pressure

Fear had kept Phil from experiencing God's pleasure so that he only felt his own pain. Because he was too self-conscious rather than aware of his own gifts, he was unable to perform under pressure, and it cost him his job.

We use that phrase "grace under pressure" or "grace under fire" to refer to someone who remains calm in the midst of trouble or turmoil. Grace under pressure implies being awake and aware of one's inner beauty and bounty of gifts. When I am graceful under pressure, I have an inner strength, a sense of integrity and the ability to name and claim the truth of my life. When I acknowledge and embrace this inner beauty, then any trouble swirling in my outer space cannot damage or deter me.

We admire people who show grace under pressure. Those who act gracefully under fire are authentic. They know who they are. They remain faithful to their dreams — to God's dreams for them — no matter how much rejection they face. I think of Joseph, the Master Dreamer, who was thrown into a well by his jealous brothers. He showed grace under pressure. The fire of his dreams would not be smothered in a dry well.

In the world of business or commerce, those who can remain calm when there are appointments to keep and calls to make and clients to see and bills to pay and presentations to prepare exhibit this quality of grace under fire. They are worth every penny they make, but they also pay a steep price. And often the cost is awareness.

True awareness allows us to see that grace and time are not enemies. They are not at war with one another. Grace doesn't say, "If I only had more time." Whether at the end of a day or the end of a life, the lament, "If I only had more time" comes from those for whom grace has been missed in the human race. Remember: It is a *human* race, not a *rat* race. This is not a race against time. Grace recognizes in whatever time one has — no matter how brief or how long — the beauty of life.

Grace implies not only a readiness but a willingness to let go — to be ready at any moment to say good-bye. Such willingness requires, like Sophia, having one's house in order, being like the battery: "ever ready." Unfortunately, most of us are more like that energized bunny that keeps going and going and going to prove to the world our worth, our stamina and our strength.

But at some point in our lives most of us realize what tired parents realize on Christmas morning when they are trying to put together the toys for their children that Santa left under the tree the night before: "Batteries not included." We feel the effects of not being as young as we once were, and we don't have the energy we once did.

For the majority of us, grace under fire becomes most apparent when the suffering we have endured has finally worn us out. It was the Greek poet Aeschylus who said, "Pain that cannot forget, falls drop by drop upon the heart, and in our sleep, against our will, comes the awful grace of God." That word "awful" implies in most contexts something terrible, something tragic. But it might also inspire something we call "awe." When we are full of awe, of wonder, we stand speechless before the divine presence. We cannot speak. We cannot even look. We are overwhelmed, immersed and enveloped by the awesome presence greater than ourselves.

This can only happen when we let go, when our hearts are broken open. Sometimes, as the ancient philosopher suggested, this process occurs over time, "drop by drop." It takes many years, like water upon a stone, to wear us down and open us up to this "awful grace."

Authentic witness comes from what we suffer. When we look at death face to face — either in our own close encounter or "close call" with mortality or in the death of someone we love — we cannot help but be changed. Our soul is softened. Tears do that. They soften the soul and break open the heart. Like a land suffering from drought, when we guard ourselves against suffering we become too dry to be of much help to anyone else. But when we open ourselves to our own experiences of pain and learn from them, we can be of great service to others.

From the Christian perspective, pain and suffering are invitations to intimacy with a God who suffers with us. The paschal mystery — the suffering, death and resurrection of Jesus — is the great reflection of God's grace. According to Eugene O'Neill in *The Great God Brown*, "The grace of God is the glue" that holds our broken hearts and shattered lives together. This is what God does for a living and for a life. This is what God lives for — to mend our broken lives. Grace is the glue that keeps our world and our personal lives from coming apart at the seams.

It is the nature of grace to ask in those moments of suffering, "What can we learn from this loss?" What can we learn from those times we have been betrayed? We could learn never to love that much again. Or we could learn never get so close to the fire for fear of getting burned again. Or we could learn to go even deeper into the mystery of love and life to see what we might find — or how we might be found.

This is the nature of grace: It provides no shelter from pain, nor does it offer avenues of escape. The Indian poet Kabir puts it like this: "If you want the truth, I will tell you the truth. Friend, listen: the God whom I love is inside." The poem from which that verse is taken is called "The Clay Jug." A poet from another time who became a prophet, Jeremiah, would appreciate the image: We are the clay, God is the potter. Though wonderfully fashionedby God, at times we become cracked pots. Sometimes hope leaks out. But more often, only when we are cracked can grace get inside.

Grace is an inside job. Though I can look outside at nature and see God's handiwork and be filled with awe at all God has made, though I can see God's grandeur in a sunrise and God's signature in a sunset, this process of sight begins within. It is called insight. If I do not have insight, I will fail to see anything.

Our True Vocation

When we look inside, we find not only our own truth but also our true vocation in life. When we were children, we were often asked, "What do you want to be when you grow up?" Notice the emphasis is on "being," not "doing." It is only when we are adults that we ask one another, "What do you *do* for a living?" But in answer to the first question, "What do you want to be," I hope our answer would be similar to the one Dom Helder Camara gave when he was interviewed by a reporter late in his life. The reporter asking the question probably thought the archbishop would reply, "I want to be a saint." But the archbishop looked at him and said, "I want to become an expert in the art of discovering the good in every person."

Could this be our true vocation in life? It would certainly make for a gracious lifestyle, a life full of grace.

What do we want to be? Do we want to be a light in the world's window or a fire in the hearth? Do we want to be a letter from home or an invitation to dinner with a friend? Why not be a call in the eventide or a walk on the beach as the tide rolls in? Who do we want to be? Contemplating the question serves to strengthen our resolve to create some inner space and cultivate a slower pace.

Albert Camus posed even more possibilities for our inner work to help us embrace the grace of our true self. "I know with certainty," Camus wrote, "that a person's work is nothing but the long journey to recover, through the detours of art, the two or three simple and great images which first gained access to his heart." We are all in the process of recovery, of trying to recover the images and stories — those moments of truth — that have served us well and given our lives meaning.

What are those moments of truth for us that reflect our true vocation? What are the stories that have shaped our lives and continue to sustain us in our inner work in being and becoming who we truly are, the beloved of God?

When we check inside, a question that may surface initially and repeatedly is another familiar one: "What are we looking for?" Are we looking for a savior or just someone to save us some time? Are we looking to be saved from sin or saved from embarrassment, shame or blame? Are we looking for a Messiah or just someone to clean up the mess? Have you noticed that, in English at least, the first syllable of Messiah is "mess"? But that's what God did — sent Jesus into the mess of our lives.

It wasn't so much to *clean up* the mess like a father, mother or maid who cleans up after the children who have "gotten into things" during their play. Jesus came to *redeem* the mess. And the only way to redeem the mess is to get down on the ground and play with the ones who are making the mess.

It is the nature of grace to help us find meaning in the mess.

Since many of our lives are defined by ragged edges of truth and loose threads of meaning, can any of us expect to have everything tied together to give to God when our time comes? We have so much unfinished business, so many things we will take care of at a later time. There are so many people we want to see, but there is so little time. With so many loose ends to pull together, isn't this the place — the sacred space of solitude and prayer — where the grace of God must come in?

Our morning prayer is the time when we give God glory for the divine inspiration of a new day and pray for the courage to be who we are, to be true to the gifts God has given us. The grace of our evening prayer offers us a kind of preparation for death even as we prepare for sleep. This is a time when we sit with the loose ends of our lives and resist the temptation to tie everything neatly together. It is at night, as we prepare for the sleep of death, that we understand Grace is the cleaning lady who comes in after a person dies and takes care of all of the unfinished business.

Grace is the seamstress who takes the loose threads of a person's life and pieces them together into a fabric called faith. We stake our lives on such images of grace because our sin is ever before us. But as our Scriptures remind us often, God is rich in mercy. Therefore, we will never feel shortchanged when it comes to grace.

It is the nature of grace to be like that credit card commercial: Grace is everywhere you want it to be. It is the nature of grace just to be. When we spend time inside, we will be prepared to see God face to face in all the places and people we meet along the way, in the good times and in the bad, in the pleasure and in the pain.

Prayer for Wisdom: A Matter of Time
A paraphrase of Psalm 90

God of all time and space,
you have been our dwelling place
in all generations.
In every situation
you are our protector and defender.
You turn us back to dust and say,
"Turn back, O children!"
For a thousand years in your sight
are like yesterday when it is past
or as a watch in the night.

I looked at my watch in the night, O God,
and it occurred to me that in ancient times
the night was divided into three watches.
Then I remembered how Jesus came to his disciples
walking on the water
around the fourth watch of the night,
just before dawn.

Don't look at your watch,
O Timeless One.
Look at me, your servant,
who always seems to be running out of time.
As your psalmist says,
all our days pass away under the heat of your gaze,
our years come to an end like a sigh.
The years of our life are threescore and ten,
or even by reason of strength, fourscore,
yet their span is toil and trouble;
they are soon gone, and we fly away.

So, teach us, O God, not to look at the face of the clock
any more than we can look at your face and live.
Teach us to number our days
that we may gain a heart of wisdom.

Chapter Three

States of Grace:
Postcards from the Edge of Time and Space

Grace...meets us where we are
But does not leave us where it found us.
—Anne Lamott

The secret of life is to enjoy the passage of time.
—James Taylor

I like this definition of grace that Anne Lamott proposes in her book *Traveling Mercies*: "Grace...meets us where we are, but does not leave us where it found us." She also defines grace "as the force that infuses our lives and keeps letting us off the hook."

I have no doubt that God keeps finding us no matter how often we hide behind hurt feelings or anger or despair. No matter how often we slip inside ourselves and discover how small our hearts really are at times. No matter how many times we go to that place filled with "pity pots" and rest inside these deep wells of feeling unappreciated or unaffirmed. God finds us. Grace meets us there.

But grace "does not leave us where it found us."

Once grace finds us she takes us deeper in the mystery of whatever we are feeling at that moment of our lives. Whatever the place is like where we find ourselves, grace takes us deeper. And then when she feels we've gone deep enough for one day — or a week or a month or however long grace thinks we can stand it — grace lets us off the hook.

I would call these different places inside our soul "states of grace." So let's visit a few of those states now and bring back for the soul, if not souvenirs, then maybe postcards from the edge of time and space.

Identifying States of Grace

One of the games we played as children to pass the time in the car on long summer vacation trips was to count license plates. As I recall, this game started soon after the question, "How long before we get there?" That means it began soon after we backed out of the driveway.

The object of the game was to see how many different states' license plates we could identify. At that time, most states' plates were functional, not fancy. Now license plates serve as billboards to advertise why the state would be a good place to visit, or its claim to fame, or its chief agricultural export.

North Carolina announces "First in Flight." Wisconsin proclaims itself "America's Dairyland." Iowa is the "Corn State," while Idaho underscores its location for "Famous Potatoes." Even if you don't know anyone in the Keystone State, "You've Got a Friend in Pennsylvania." Vermont has "Green Mountains," but Arkansas is the "Natural State." New Mexico invites people to explore its "Land of Enchantment," Arizona its "Grand Canyon" and Alaska the "Last Frontier."

For the past few years I've lived in the "Land of Lincoln," but since I grew up in Missouri my soul still has its share of skepticism; so if you want me to believe something, you have to "Show Me."

My first assignment as a priest was in Centerville, Iowa. When I introduced myself the first Sunday I was there, I said that my last name rhymes with "Razzle Dazzle." So that year for Christmas, I received a new license plate with "Razzle" emblazoned upon it. These kinds of plates are called "vanity" plates. They cost more than regular plates, but the good thing about them is that in this day and age when most cars look alike, they make it easier to find one's car in a crowded parking lot.

Although I left Iowa almost twenty years ago and have had numerous plates from different states on various cars since then, I still have that Iowa "Razzle" plate. It reminds me of my first three years of public ministry with people who taught me, loved me, challenged me and forgave me for my youthful mistakes. That old license plate is infused with special meaning and memories. It's a sacred souvenir of a time, a place and a people I will never forget. It serves as a relic of a time when people in a state of grace known as Iowa showed me the face of God.

Maybe I'm guilty of belonging to a "pack rat" club, but that "Razzle" relic reflects a ritual that nourishes the soul. All the places we visit, whether for vacation or because of our vocation, can offer us a piece of real estate known as "holy ground." When we are aware of God's presence in the places and people we meet along the way, we know we are traveling in a state called Grace.

The Sacredness of All Things

When I am on the road giving retreats and missions, I rarely come back empty-handed. I may bring back wooden crosses made by an eighty-year old woodcarver in Iowa or a refrigerator magnet of a lighthouse that serves as the landmark of a town in Michigan or a shell from Newport Beach in Rhode Island or a bottle of homemade raspberry wine from Wisconsin. I often come back with a rock or two from the place where I visited to remind me of the "living stones" I met in the state of grace I visited.

In the language of grace, all is gift. Everything is infused with the presence of God. Grace transfigures all faces and transforms all places. This is the power of grace at work. It's not about which is more important — grace or good works. It's about grace at work. The call of grace is to see the greatness of God in the smallest things. It is to revel in the glory of God in the radiant love of those we meet on this odyssey of life.

But as we travel through life, do we see ourselves as pilgrims or tourists? When we move as tourists, we want to make every minute count and take in as much as possible. We take pictures or buy postcards to remind us of the beauty or the history of the place that makes it a tourist attraction, but then we move on to another place because we don't want to miss anything. After all, the next place where we stop may be even more breathtaking. On the other hand, when we move as a pilgrim, we acknowledge from the start that there is something beautiful up ahead that may take our breath away, but we take our time, catch our breath and etch each sight in the scrapbook we call the soul.

As tourists, we may never be satisfied with where we are because there must be something better around the bend. As pilgrims, however, we are where we are, and wherever we are is a good place to be. When we realize that each place where we stand or sit or sleep or tell a story or listen to a tale of wonder or of woe is a state of grace, then we will come to know our lives like the "back of our hands."

When we say we know a place "like the back of our hand," we know the place well. Those who are able to give us direction in life are those who know the place where they stand like the back of their hand. Those who know the paths to heaven know the paths of earth; they know the place where they stand, the place where they live, is charged with divine light. The street lamps on this odyssey are lit by God's grace.

Many of us keep looking for this light somewhere else. We look for fulfillment at another place, in another time. But our challenge is to see grace in this place, right here, right now. The streets where we walk today are bright as the paths of heaven because we illuminate them with the light of the divine presence within us. If we don't find this grace where we are right now, we will not find it anywhere. It is inside us: This is the one place where we will find God's grace. Here we can study the "back of our hands" and know this place as if for the first time.

But be aware that when we enter this solitary space of the soul, we are advised to leave our watches, alarm clocks, sundials, hourglasses — whatever devices we use to tell time — at the door, because when we look within we don't tell time anything. Time tells us.

No Time To Be On Time

When I was growing up, Mom always set the clocks at home five minutes fast. I'm not sure why. Maybe it gave us a sense that we had less time than we did. Or maybe she was teaching us to show up early and never be late. When looking at the clock in the kitchen, Mom would say, "It's five minutes fast," and I would realize I had five more minutes than I thought I did. Every minute counts.

When those two words *on time* are flashed on airport monitors to tell passengers the status of their flights or to inform families when the plane carrying a loved one is scheduled to arrive, those two words are good news. When the word *delayed* is flashed on the screen, frustration is fueled. And when the word *cancelled* comes on the monitor, anger is likely to erupt. Transpose the word *on* in the phrase *on time* and you get *no time*. Those two words, *no time*, describe the state of most people in society today.

If we spend our time watching the clock or being controlled by the clock or always seem to be running out of time or never having enough time, blame the Benedictines. By inventing the liturgy of the hours, stopping at eight points during the day to pray, the monks gave us the gift of clocks. The word *clock* comes from the Latin word meaning *bell*, since the monks designated the hours of prayer by ringing a bell.

How do we experience time — as a circle or a line? If we view time as a circle, it has no beginning or end. Eastern cultures and religious traditions view time in this way. But for most of us in the West, time is a line: a timeline. It has starting point: "In the beginning" (Genesis 1: 1) — and a stopping point: "It is finished" (John 19: 30). We mark on this time line our past, our present and our future. We speak of time in terms of yesterday, today and tomorrow.

Some of us may also think of time as a spiral. Time spirals upward as it flies or down when it drags. When time is up, we mean there is no more time left to take the test. Isn't it interesting how we use words to describe time? When time flies, one would think time is up — it's a bird, it's a plane, it's a blimp! But actually time is up when it spirals down and reaches the point of extinction: There is no more time.

We are so conscious of time. Minute by minute, we count on time to tell us what we should do, where we should go, whether we're on time or late and have to wait at the gate. Many blame the Industrial Revolution and recent advances in technology for this preoccupation with time. The assembly line, the eight-hour day and the forty-hour week, punching a time clock, watching the clock, looking forward to the whistle blowing — all came with the sound of time ticking away.

Our ancestors told time by looking at the sky and the position of the sun or the moon. These days, who has time to look outside?

As we travel through the various stages of life, the marriage of time and space encourages us not only to look within but also outside ourselves. We know we are in a state of grace when we can look up and see the stars. We are in a state of grace when we look around and see the folks who form the circle of our family and friends — in whose caring circumference we feel safe. We are in a state of grace when we look down and see the good earth on which we stand; or if we're up in the air, we see the ground on which there are no boundaries. Isn't it true than when viewed from above there are no state lines or borders? All the earth is a state of grace.

But turf is not the only thing we divide with a line. We also draw a line in the sands of time. There is the ritual of documenting times of birth and death on certificates. We are very precise when documenting a lifespan on earth. We point to the minute. A doctor will say, "Time of death: 12:37 A.M." Or recall the story of the woman giving birth to twins on December 31, 1999, around midnight. Evidently she held the view that 2000 and not 2001 was the beginning of the new millennium because she asked for a C-section so that one baby was delivered at 11:59 P.M. on December 31, 1999, and the second baby arrived after midnight on January 1, 2000. Twins born in two different years — in different centuries and even millenniums. Time is such a thin line, only a second, but it is a dividing line. Every minute counts.

We are not so precise, of course, when we etch time on a stone. I don't recall ever seeing a tombstone that had the exact times of a person's birth and death. Some round it off to years; most at least give the day, month and year of the birth and death dates, but never hours or minutes. In matters of life and death, minutes are crucial. Yet in the end they don't count as much as days. One notable exception is the monument to the victims of the Oklahoma City bombing on April 19, 1995, which is eloquent in its simplicity. It has the time the bomb exploded, 9:03, engraved in stone.

However we measure time, there is no doubt that time flies. We just pray that whenever it comes down, time has a safe landing. And it will when we view time as a dreammaker rather than a dictator. When the clock controls us, time dictates our every move. But when we view wherever we are as a state of grace, time is free; the clock loses its power to control, so we don't need to "save time."

Spend It, Don't Save It

At the turn of the new millennium, we buried a time capsule at the place where I live. In one sense, a time capsule is an attempt to "save time." These are the times of our lives. The best and the worst, I suppose. We try to save this time and give it as a gift to future generations. But if we are honest, we put in the time capsule the good times but also the bad: the promise and the pain, the joy and the sorrow. All come together to mark the time of our lives.

Time measured by the clock is different from time marked on a calendar. Clocks measure time by the sweep of hands across the face, while for calendars an X marks the spot when a day is done. Those sentenced to so many days in jail may mark Xs on the calendar. Those sentenced to too many days on earth may cross off days at a time.

The best we can do is listen to our lives. Hear its truth. What is my life telling me? Am I bored? Am I excited? Am I in pain?

It is said that Herman Melville had the following quote over the place where he wrote: "Be true to the dreams of thy youth." Have we been true? Have we discovered our truth — our reason for living?

When we see time only as a dictator instead of a dreammaker, it is easy to lose track of our dreams. It's as easy as it is to lose track of time. And when we lose track of our dreams, we fall into ruts. Life becomes routine. Function becomes a substitute for fun. Habits replace experiments. "Try and fail" becomes "We tried that and it didn't work." This is a clear sign that one is growing old: We begin to fall into habits. Indeed, we need certain routines in our lives that serve as daily rituals of regularity. They keep us rooted. Yet notice the direction of the regularity: fall. We don't rise to routines — we fall into them. And at a certain point, routines become ruts.

When we are forever running in the "rat race," we can't help but make ruts. The finish line for the rat race is a hole in the wall or a hole in the ground. This is where the dreams of our youth go to be buried.

But the grace of spending time in the company of a friend on a warm summer evening is to touch the dreams of our youth again. When we have been hurt in a relationship or a friendship has failed, it is possible to cover up our dreams of intimacy with the dust of our resentment. And when we lose track of our dreams, we lose track of our souls.

While holding fast to the dreams of our youth, it is also important to honor the process of growing old. No matter how many wrinkles wrap our faces with "wisdom rings," we need not grow less passionate about our lives and our dreams. When we have a friend or two to remind us of our dreams, there is still a future full of hope.

When we find a safe place to tell a part of or even our whole story, we spend time in a place called grace. It takes time to share our truth with someone we can trust, but it also affords an intimacy that nourishes soul. Truth telling is a spiritual exercise, and when we tell someone the truth we are in a state of grace.

Time Travel: Lessons from the Road

Here is a piece of my truth that I frame in an incident that happened many years ago. When I was growing up, my older brother Ed owned a motorcycle. It wasn't a Harley Davidson or one of the big machines with lots of power that makes a lot of noise. It was a smaller bike — a Yamaha, I think — but it certainly made more noise and had more power than the bicycle I was used to. For my bicycle to make noise, I had to put baseball cards in the spokes! I think I was a sophomore in high school when Ed brought home his latest bike. I asked if I could take it for a spin. Since I didn't have my driver's license yet, Ed said I could ride it in the half-acre field that was parallel to our yard. I jumped on that motorcycle, gave it some gas and took off!

It was clear from the outset that I wasn't giving the motorcycle a spin, it was taking me for a ride!

My family will never forget the look on our neighbors' faces as they saw me coming toward them. It was a beautiful Saturday afternoon in early summer, and they were sitting in lawn chairs outside their house. But they were not sitting for long when they saw me on that motorcycle speeding straight at them. They jumped out of their chairs and scattered. Lawn chairs were flying everywhere as they raced to get out of the way! I didn't know how to stop the motorcycle that was now taking me on the ride of my life. And if I crashed into the neighbor's house, this would likely be my last ride!

I jumped off the motorcycle, and the bike came to a gasping, grinding halt on the ground, spinning its wheels. Except for a severely bruised ego, I was unhurt. To this day, whenever I am tempted to get on a high horse — or when my dad feels I need a dose of humility — the story of the runaway motorcycle makes its way into the conversation. It is a story I would rather forget, but the truth is I need to remember it.

The truth the story tells me is that I don't do well when I have more power than I can handle. Inevitably, I have to jump off, and the power source spins out of control and crashes.

For most of us, when we have a scare, a close brush with death, or experience a tragedy of some kind in our family, we are stopped in our tracks. Certainly when someone we love dies or we catch a glimpse of the face of death, time stands still. The world may keep spinning, but our world stops. We focus all of our attention on the one who has died. Death stops us in our tracks.

One of the lessons I cling to from that wild ride on the bike is that maybe life should stop us in our tracks, too.

Anna: The Gift of Tears

Several years ago I gave a mission at a parish in a Chicago suburb. After one of my morning conferences at the mission, an elderly woman who told me her name was Anna asked to speak with me. Her thick accent prompted an obvious question. "Where are you from?" I asked. "Hungary," she said, but she told me she'd been in the Chicago area for more than thirty years. Still, her voice carried echoes of the land from which she came.

Anna told me bits and pieces of her story. She skipped many years from the time she arrived in this country with her husband more than thirty years ago to the landmark moment that occurred the year before our conversation and continued to shape her days into an endless night. "My husband died," Anna said. The pain of this loss was still so close to the surface that she began to cry. The grief over the death of her husband of forty-seven years hung over Anna like a gray cloud that threatens rain at any time. The downpour lasted only a few moments. The handkerchief was ready to dry her tears, but the pain was still close. How much Anna loved her husband, and how much she missed him.

The last morning of that mission was Ash Wednesday. Anna came up to me again and handed me a gift. There were more tears in her eyes as she said, "I want you to remember me." And then Anna leaned very close to me and whispered a piece of her story she had left unspoken when we talked a couple days before. "Please pray for me. I have breast cancer." Terror and tears filled Anna's eyes. She felt alone. She was facing this illness alone. I held her for just a moment, but I wanted to enfold her and not let go. Then she walked out into the bright sunlight of that Ash Wednesday morning more than three years ago.

In just the two brief times we visited, I was taken by Anna's deep faith. I was certain her faith would help her ride through the storm of illness and loss. But facing the darkness caused by the diagnosis of cancer so soon after burying her husband was difficult indeed. At that parish mission, I saw Anna's gift of tears. She was not afraid to cry and to share her pain with a stranger such as me. Anna touched my weary soul during that mission three years ago. I promised her I would pray with her, that I would not forget her. And she made it easy to keep the memory of her alive. She gave me a gift — a picture of Budapest, the city of her birth. When I looked at the picture under the light of the bright sun, I noticed a smudge, a fingerprint. Anna had left her fingerprint on the picture — and upon my heart.

When I returned to the parish for another mission three years later, Anna came up to me and asked, "Do you remember me?" "Of course, I remember you," I said. I reminded her of the picture of her beloved Budapest that I had placed on my prayer table during that season of ashes three years before. But I confess that I almost didn't recognize her, because this time she was smiling, not crying. There were no tears. Her cancer had been in remission for two years. Anna had been given a new lease on life, and her face radiated hope and peace. Anna was beaming with redeeming grace.

Anna's journey of faith reflects our own odyssey through various states of grace. In the death of her husband and her battle with cancer, Anna had been taken on a journey deep into the paschal mystery. She allowed that reality to find a place in her. This is what we are invited to do in these various states of grace: to leave some room so that the paschal mystery can have its place, its way, its *holy* way, with us. When we create such space, we begin to see that this is the very place where our hope is born.

This journey into the soul where the paschal mystery finds a home in our hearts mirrors the journey of Jesus — not only his journey to Jerusalem, where he would suffer and die, but also the journey from heaven to earth. This is the journey Paul describes in his famous hymn to the Philippians when he speaks about Jesus: "Though he was in the form of God, he did not deem equality with God something to be grasped at" (Philippians 2: 6). Instead, we believe that Jesus "emptied himself and took the form of a slave, being born in human likeness." Paul sums up Jesus' journey in these terms: "He was known to be of human estate, and it was thus that he humbled himself, obediently accepting death, death on a cross!" (2: 8).

Because Jesus did not "deem equality with God something to be grasped at but emptied himself," this make us "redeemable."

Though our sins may be like scarlet, we are redeemable.

Though we run away in fear, hide in shame, cover up our blame, we are redeemable.

Though our pain is more than we can bear at times and our guilt is more than we can hold, we are redeemable. We need only ask God to give us the grace to empty ourselves of those attitudes that keep us from loving like Jesus. When we do, we find that place within where the paschal mystery takes root and hope can grow. Finding this place within will allow our faces to radiate God's redeeming grace. When the paschal mystery finds a place within us, we find an inner strength that reminds us that "God is our help" and that we will never experience disgrace. We have seen this paschal mystery of faith etched on the faces of those who have survived tragedies of every sort without yielding to despair. We have heard this paschal mystery of faith proclaimed in the voices of those who have suffered and say to us, "I would have never made it without my faith." We have felt this paschal mystery of faith in the embrace of those who have come to be with us in our pain and our loss. They come not with answers or explanations or pious predictions about how things will get better. They come because they have found that place of the paschal mystery in their own souls and stories, have tasted their own tears, know their own fears. Still, they believe they are redeemable. These are the people who, like Jesus, empty themselves so that God may fill them with the fullness of divine life.

These are the people who have stood in that dark, damp state of grace where the light has grown dim and tears have fallen like rain, who are filled with a light that is not their own. People like Anna. As I completed the second mission, she gave me another gift — a small tablecloth she embroidered with bright, colorful flowers. We used Anna's gift on the altar during Holy Week — another souvenir of the soul gained while visiting a state of grace.

Show Us the Way

As we travel through various states of grace in the course of our lives, this much seems clear to me: Only when I acknowledge that I don't know where I'm going will grace be able to show me the way. Only when I realize I don't have all the answers, will grace grant me a question that will lead me in hope. Only when I affirm the endless transitions of my life, will grace transport me to a place of peace.

"There is a day," Wendell Berry writes, "when the road neither comes nor goes, and the way is not a way but a place." On this grace odyssey may we arrive at such a place and enjoy our stay.

Grace abounds around us and within us. As the poet William Stafford wrote, "I am saved in this big world by unforeseen friends, or times when only a glance from a passenger beside me, or just the tired branch of a willow inclining toward earth, may teach me how to join earth and sky." Earth and sky were forever joined when Jesus came down to earth. The spirit Jesus left behind when he rose from the dead and ascended to heaven — going back to the place from which he had come and from which he will come again — means we can live each day in a state of grace.

State of Grace: A Matter of Space
Based on Psalm 91

I hear the echoes of Jacob when he saw
the stairway to heaven:
"Truly God is in this spot,"
although he did not recognize the Divine Presence.

How often, O God,
have I found myself in a certain space
and failed to take off my shoes
because I did not see you in that place?

Wherever I am, wherever I go,
I dwell, O Loving One, in the shelter of your arms.
I abide in the shadow of your care,
for you are my refuge and my fortress.

This is where wisdom begins
and life ends: trust in God.
I know you will deliver me from those who want to do me harm;
from deceitful and cunning snares you will spare my life.

As I travel through the endless states of grace
where there are no boundaries or limits to your love,
you say, "Fear not the terror of the night,
nor the arrow that flies by day."

Your angels guide and guard me,
O Gracious One.
With their hands they bear me up and lift me free,
lest I catch my foot upon a stone.

When I call to you seeking direction,
you answer me.
You protect me and show me the way
to the safest place of all: home.

Chapter Four

A Geography of Grace: Finding a Safe Place

A holy place is a place where we speak in whispers,
Our words become prayers and our heart falls down
And rises up again.
—Lakota Sioux

We have failed to live up to our geography.
—Theodore Roethke

In exploring various states of grace, we noted how this odyssey takes us on an inner journey. This is what we might call the geography of grace as we seek to find and rest and rendezvous with God in that sacred space we call the soul.

What is the nature of a sacred space? It is a place where we feel safe enough to take off our shoes — and maybe more. It is a place where the naked truth is spoken, reverenced and heard. It is a place where we can be ourselves and don't have to pretend we're someone else. It is a place where we can make ourselves at home with God. When we find this sacred space, we seek to reflect this inner space in our "outer" space by creating safe places where others can encounter the presence of God.

Archbishop Desmond Tutu described this geography of grace when he was in St. Louis a few years ago to accept the Global Citizen Award given by the University of Missouri at St. Louis. In his talk, he described what had happened in South Africa the past few years as the "third way" of ending oppression. The first way, Tutu said, is for victims to claim vengeance as their right. This way is captured in the ancient truth often used by opponents of the death penalty: "An eye for an eye makes the world blind." But Tutu said the second way — to "brush the past aside" — doesn't work either in personal or global disputes. "You can't paper over offenses and look the other way," he said.

Tutu explained that the third way involves listening, prayer and forgiveness. "In South Africa we tried a third way, looking the beast in the eye," he said. "We used confession and forgiveness." Tutu noted that when President Nelson Mandela appointed him to lead South Africa's Truth and Reconciliation Commission in 1995, he and the other commissioners "listened to and investigated charges of human rights violations and in some cases granted amnesty — even for terrible atrocities — in exchange for the truth." This process of reconciliation would not have been possible for the members of this commission, Tutu said, without prayer, which "gave them the grace to forgive one another by listening to each other's heart-wrenching stories." When we follow this third way, Tutu said, we "need to sit down in a safe place and tell each other the pain that is in the pit of our hearts."

In the geography of grace, contemplative prayer creates a safe place within the cave of our hearts. In this prayer of listening, we draw on the grace of God to give us the courage to "tell each other the pain that is in the pit of our hearts."

The way to peace, this path to that safe place, is not paved with good intentions but with the truth that sets us free.

This way to peace is not a private drive; it is an expansive avenue that leads to our common ground. Our common ground is this: the suffering we have all experienced. We go deeper into the mystery of this suffering — the paschal mystery — when we enter the cave of our hearts in silent prayer. In this sacred stillness before the divine presence, we encourage those parts of ourselves that are "far off" to come near and sit for a spell. We extend hospitality toward those parts of our lives that we name as our sin, those attitudes that cause us to be ill at ease, those actions that are irreconcilable with who we are. They all come together in this sacred space of the soul to tell us their truth.

A Scary, Sacred Silence

This way that leads to the cave of our hearts directs us out of those places in our world that we have divided into tiny chunks of real estate. When we find this sacred space within ourselves, we invite others to spend some time with us in the silence and find some common ground. It is this expansive avenue of grace that takes us away from our "turf" — those places in our lives that we think are safe because we've constructed walls and barricades and barriers to keep others outside — and leads to true peace. From this stance of sacred stillness, we listen for the truth. And the truth is that though our differences are "real," the "estate" belongs to God.

In the geography of grace, when we arrive at this sacred space of silent prayer, we reverence each one's gifts, breathe on each one's wounds and respect each one's story.

In our public expressions of prayer we often voice our petitions or intercessions, and after each petition we say, "God, hear us" or "God, hear our prayer" as if we suspect God isn't listening. Or we think God doesn't know what we need until we ask. We plead with God, bend the divine ear, try to break God's heart with our words, our stories of woe, our pain and our problems. We do this as if God is not paying attention to our problems.

But if we believe that God knows what we need before we ask, why don't we just be quiet? Why don't we just inwardly open the whole of our situation to the divine reality? Why don't we stop stringing along endless words and just listen to God in the silence? Is it because we are afraid of the silence?

The silence reveals that there are no answers. Some events in life are so crushing no words can capture the experience. We stand before our God in this sacred but uncomfortable space of silence, trying to pray.

But there are no answers. There is only the prayer. There is only silence.

In looking at the landscape of the soul in the geography of grace, it makes a difference in how we understand prayer. If we do all the talking, heaping empty phrase upon empty phrase — even if these phrases sing God's praises — when will we experience the silence that gives God a chance to speak? If we are still and we don't hear the voice of God, we are tempted to fill up the emptiness with even more empty phrases and words.

God knows what we need. The more time we spend in silence in the sacred space of the soul, the less fear we will feel as we explore the geography of grace. When we are not afraid of the silence, our practice of prayer will not rely on words but rather encourage us to sit on the edge of what Thomas Merton described as that great "abyss opening up in the center of your soul." Have we seen this abyss inside our soul? Have we danced around its edges, spoken of its danger, listened to its silence, been swallowed by its hunger?

This abyss of solitude, Merton wrote, "will never be satisfied with any created thing." It is a hunger than can only be filled by God.

When There's Not Enough Room

Only when we spend time in our "inner space," the cave of our hearts, listening to God's Word, listening to each other's story, listening to the beating of our own hearts, can we begin to create safe places in our "outer space." But difficult as it is to create some sacred space in the inner landscape, it is even harder to create or even find safe places in the world. Schools were once thought to be safe places, but then there was Columbine and so many other schools where violence killed our youth and shattered our illusions. Even more, the terrorist attacks of September 11, 2001, imploded our sense of security at going to our workplace or even walking down the street.

Some look at these scenes of violence in our schools and see them as evidence that we are running out of time — the end of the world must be near. But I look at them and see we are running out of room.

There is a scene in the book of Genesis that captures well this sense of space and what happens when we feel we don't have enough room. We learn that "Abram was very rich in cattle, in silver, and in gold" (13: 2), and that "Lot, who went with Abram, also had flocks and herds and tents" (13: 5). These two had so much that "the land could not support both of them dwelling together, for their possessions were so great they could not live together" (13: 6). The conflict that resulted from having too many possessions and too little room causes Abram to say, "Let there be no strife between you and me...for we are kindred" (13: 8).

His solution to this strife is to separate. So Lot turned his eyes to the east and "saw that the plain of the Jordan was well watered...like the garden of the Lord" (13: 10). Memories of Eden etched deep in his psyche may have caused Lot to look eastward. There was enough water to sustain his herd, enough space for him and his kin to pitch their many tents.

Abram, on the other hand, looked up. "Lift up your eyes," God says to Abram, "look from the place where you are." God tells the patriarch to "look in every direction — for all the land that you see I will give to you and your offspring forever" (13: 14-15). God is offering Abram wide-open spaces on which oto settle his clan. "Arise," God says, "walk through the length and breadth of the land, for I will give it to you" (13: 17).

We have Lot settling in a land that looked a lot like Eden and Abram building an altar to God "by the oaks of Mamre" in a land that stretches as far as the eye can see. In thinking about these wide-open spaces, the question arises, Where is our sacred space? Where is that place in our lives with which we are so identified? Is it a wide-open space or a narrow place? Is it a closet or a coliseum? Is it a place that has an open door or a closed shutter? When we are in this sacred space of ours, do we paint the landscape with bright colors of hope or with shades of gray? Is our space vibrant with life or drab and dreary, drawn with bleak tones of black and white? Is it space with which we are so identified that when another passes by and we are not there, they notice our absence?

Like Abram, when we find our space, do we build an altar there to designate that this is a sacred space? Or, like Lot, do we look for a space that resembles Eden? Abram built an altar to honor God's call in his life. Building an altar is a continuous theme in Scripture to reflect a place of revelation. It denotes for all time and for all to see that on this site something significant occurred: Something holy happened here — there has been a moment of truth and grace.

But also remember why Abram and Lot had to split up. There wasn't enough room for both of them. No matter how wide the land or how much space they had, there wasn't enough room because they had too many possessions. The story says we need enough space to move around. If our lives are too cramped, we can't move, we can't breathe. I once lived in a community house where there wasn't enough room. There were enough *rooms*, just not enough room for some of us to live under the same roof. Some of us carried too much baggage, held on tightly to opposing ideologies; there wasn't enough room for a different point of view.

Sometimes our minds become so narrow that there's not enough room to change our minds. When our hearts become this small, it's time to move and look for some higher ground. Or is it lower — as in taking the lowest place? Whichever it is, when there's not enough room in the geography of grace, we are not in a safe place.

Instead, we find ourselves caught somewhere between a blessing and a curse.

Between a Blessing and a Curse

This is the place where I find myself, for example, when I hear Luke's version of the Beatitudes (6: 17-26). I'm not really poor, but I'm far from rich. I've never been so hungry that I've worried about my next meal, but I've experienced other hungers, more of the soul than the stomach. Regarding the blessing and the curse of those who weep and those who laugh, well, I could be anywhere between those two poles depending on what day it is. And though I've experienced some rejection, the truth is I want people to speak well of me.

So, I am caught somewhere between a blessing and a curse, wonder and woe.

A few years ago I saw the film *Entertaining Angels* — the story of Dorothy Day, Peter Maurin and the founding of the Catholic Worker Movement. I was struck how they walked the fine line, the treacherous terrain, between a blessing and a curse. In one scene, Dorothy comes into the room and watches as Peter washes the foot of an old man whose shoes are so worn that they would fall off his feet if not for the string that holds them together. Without a word, Dorothy sits down, takes off the string that holds the man's other shoe together, and begins to wash that foot. Then Peter takes off his own shoes and gives them to the old man. "Peter, what are you going to do for shoes?" Dorothy asks. He smiles, shrugs and walks away.

The same day I saw the movie, I went to the Plaza — an upscale shopping area in Kansas City — to browse at the Barnes & Noble bookstore. As I was waiting to cross the street, I saw a man sitting on the sidewalk. This was his space — whether it was "sacred" or not is open for discussion. I had seen this same man at this same spot many times before and regarded him more as a pest and a panhandler than one of the poor that Jesus praises in the Gospels. Waiting for the cars to pass, I thought to myself: "How am I going to get into the bookstore without being accosted by this man for some money?" But the light changed and the traffic stopped before I had a chance to devise a strategy of avoiding this guy. I crossed the street.

"How are you doing today, sir?" he said.

"I'm fine." I reached into my pocket. "How are you?"

"Not so good today. I hurt my foot." I looked down at his shoes. They were replicas of the shoes I had seen earlier in the movie about Dorothy Day.

"That's too bad," I said, still intent to get inside the safe refuge of books. I handed him a dollar. The man looked at the dollar and said, "Bless you, sir."

I walked into the store, still caught somewhere between a blessing and a curse.

When I returned home, I put a dollar bill on my prayer table. The words written on the back of our money became my mantra for a while: "In God We Trust."

Isn't it interesting that our currency calls us to conversion? But then, if what they say is true — that time is money — maybe creating these safe and sacred places in the world is less about money and more about time. How much time do we have?

More than anything, creating these safe spaces is about trust. Where do we place our trust — in the Almighty Dollar or in Almighty God? Our Almighty Dollar tells us to trust in Almighty God. This is the theme of Luke's version of the Beatitudes. Jesus' prophetic words demand we place our trust in God or suffer the consequences. So how do we move to that higher ground of trust? Or is it lower ground? After all, the poor are not the high and mighty but the down and out. They are normally found sitting on the ground, on sidewalks and street corners, in alleys and gullies, looking up to those who pass by. At least this is the movement that Luke makes clear in his map of the Beatitudes.

If you recall, Matthew's map has Jesus going up a mountain, like Moses on Sinai, and teaching the disciples a new way of living. But in Luke, "Jesus *came down* with his disciples and stood on a level place." Then Jesus *looked up* at his disciples and began to show them how to walk this fine line between a blessing and a curse, wonder and woe.

Jesus looked up at them: He taught them not from a pedestal but from a level plain. In the geography of grace, this is the first step we take when we are caught somewhere between a blessing and a curse: Find the lowest place.

This is what Jesus does in Luke's Gospel: He levels the praying field so that all — the poor and rich, the hungry and full, the sorrowful and the joyful, the sick and the healthy — might find their home on the map of God's mercy. Though Jesus identifies himself with the poor — and unlike Matthew it is not the "poor in spirit" but simply the materially poor that Luke is referring to — Jesus isn't condemning those who have made a fortune in this world. He is just reminding them of what we all know: Money cannot buy true joy, nor can it purchase everlasting life. Indeed, in the pattern of Mary's song of praise, the Magnificat, which appears earlier in the Gospel, Luke is drawing a map where the poor are lifted up and the rich are sent empty away as a prophetic way to call forth conversion.

Walking this fine line between a blessing and a curse will ultimately lead to a crossroads: "Blessed are you when people hate you, when they exclude you, revile you, and defame you on account of me." In the film about Dorothy Day, there is the scene in which the Cardinal of New York comes to the Catholic Worker House to confront Dorothy about her activities. The cardinal applauds her efforts to feed the poor but is concerned about her writing and protesting for social justice. Dorothy says to the cardinal, "When we give food and shelter to the poor, we are called saints; when we confront the injustices that cause poverty, we are called communists. We are neither."

Dorothy Day often found herself somewhere between a blessing and a curse.

Jesus the Panhandler

Reflecting on the man that I saw on the street outside the bookstore, the thought comes to me: So what if he was a panhandler? The word "panhandler" comes from the French word meaning "extended forearm." The poor stretch out their arms hoping someone will respond to their needs. Jesus stretched out his arms on a cross and with his "extended forearms" gave forgiveness to a world begging for mercy. It is this plain, this simple: We are all beggars in need of God's mercy.

Or we might look at that word "panhandler" through Spanish eyes. The Spanish word for bread is *pan*. Maybe a panhandler is one who handles bread. Jesus the Panhandler "took bread in his hands, blessed and broke it and said, 'This is my body'" (Luke 22: 19).

There is another meaning to that word "pan." It means, "to wash earth, gravel or other material in a pan in search of gold." When we fail to reach a dream or finish a project or find the gold in life, we say, "It didn't pan out." Often when we find ourselves caught somewhere between a blessing and a curse, things don't pan out.

On this grace odyssey we might imagine ourselves panning for gold in a stream. In truth, all of us are panhandlers when we journey through the land of grace. We stretch out our hands begging God's mercy and healing. In this moment of truth we stretch out our hands in a balancing act as we walk the tightrope between a blessing and a curse.

The prophet Jeremiah (17: 5-8) describes this stream and some of the other features of this landscape we encounter in this geography of grace. According to the prophet, in the land of grace we can sink our roots deep into the soil of trust. The prophet's image is of a "tree planted by water, sending out its roots by the stream" (17: 5-8). The geography of grace takes into consideration the temperature and the topology of the soul. In this safe place, this place of grace, we stay green with hope even when the heat of rejection threatens to wither our commitment. We learn how not to fear or be anxious when the sky remains stoical, withholding its tears. In this place of grace, we may be thirsty but find our refreshment from deep beneath the soil where the waters of the nearby stream make the ground moist. Thus, even in those most dangerous, drought-stricken times of our lives, we still bear fruit.

We've been to this stream now and then. We've sipped from this stream and found our thirst quenched and our soul moistened. That stream where we sift for gold may be a sidewalk along a busy street where a man with worn shoes and aching feet begs for money. That stream may be a soup kitchen line where hungry people shuffle along feeling far from blessed. That stream may be the house down the street where a person is sick or the home of a friend who is weeping and grieving the loss of a loved one.

In the geography of grace, when we're caught somewhere between a blessing and a curse, it all comes down to trust in God. This is the way, the only way, to that life-giving stream.

As we walk this fine line between wonder and woe, if we fall we will always land in the lap of luxury known as the grace and mercy of God. It is the same safe place described on our currency: "In God We Trust." Isn't it strange that we put those words on our money and not on our memory? For only when we inscribe those words on our soul will God be able to buy for us and our world a future full of hope.

Avoid the Mainstream

When walking by this stream through graceland, however, there is one caution: Beware of the mainstream. It is so easy to compromise in this culture of ours rather than confront the erosion of values. Most of us like to be in the mainstream, not on the margin. We like to see ourselves in the center rather than on the cutting edge.

In Luke's version of the Beatitudes, Jesus implies that those who live in the reign of God necessarily live on the edge. On this grace odyssey we don't merely trod the path of conformity, but rather we walk on the trail of transformation.

In a culture caught in the vice of violence, we dare to practice peace.

In a culture where so many are excluded, we dare to be inclusive.

In a culture where compassion fatigue seems to have reached epidemic proportions, we dare to be there for those crushed by indifference.

This is not a "pie in the sky" kind of faith. It is not a belief that if we just endure the pain and suffering in this life, heaven will take our pain away. No, this is a radical and redemptive belief in the presence of the wounded but resurrected Christ alive in our midst. It is a firm faith, a stubborn, sacred conviction that Christ is walking with us on this journey of transformation.

Trust in God demands that we focus the eyes of our hearts on those who walk this way with us — especially when they are pushed aside or stepped upon or left for dead by the side of the road. People who trust in God have tasted their tears, but rather than choking on them, they swallow hope instead.

Jesus knew firsthand the risks of walking on the edge. Indeed, Luke's version of the Beatitudes may flow from Jesus' experience of being rejected by his own family and friends earlier in the Gospel (4: 16-30). After his forty-day retreat in the desert, Jesus begins his preaching, teaching and healing ministry, "and his reputation spread throughout the region" (4: 14). When he returns to his hometown to deliver his "inaugural address," he quotes his favorite prophet, Isaiah (61: 1-2):

> *The Spirit of God is upon me:*
> *Therefore God has anointed me.*
> *God has sent me to bring glad tidings to the poor,*
> *to proclaim liberty to captives,*
> *recovery of sight to the blind and release to prisoners,*
> *to announce a year of favor from God.*

The reaction of the people to what is essentially Jesus' mission statement is mixed. At first, when Jesus says this passage "is fulfilled in your hearing," people "spoke favorably of him; they marveled at the appealing discourse which came from his lips" (Luke 4: 21-22). But it isn't long before they begin to question Jesus' credentials.

Jesus' experience in Nazareth reminds me of how when I'm on the road, I sometimes notice that certain towns proudly proclaim their favorite sons and daughters who have made a name for themselves and the town. From astronauts to actors, from presidents to pundits, from sports heroes to cartoon characters, small towns and sometimes large cities proudly display the name of a hometown hero who has claimed a measure of fame.

On an interstate in Iowa, there's a sign that says, "The birthplace of John Wayne." On a stretch of I-55 in Illinois, a sign notes the birthplace and boyhood home of Ronald Reagan. On I-70 near downtown St. Louis, Mark McGwire has a stretch of the highway named after him. Kansas City has named a mile of the same interstate that runs along its stadium complex in honor of George Brett. Chester, a small town in southern

Illinois, advertises itself as the hometown of Popeye "the sailor man." There is no mention of the love of his life, Olive.

My guess is that after the incident in the Gospel when Jesus returns home and preaches to his family, friends and neighbors, they are not going to put up a sign that says, "Welcome to Nazareth: Boyhood home of Jesus." In fact, just the opposite reaction happens: They run him out of town and threaten to throw him over a cliff.

What was his crime? Was it fame and its aftereffects? Indeed, he had made a name for himself as a healer, but he could now work no miracles in his own backyard because of their lack of faith.

Was it the fact that he was Joseph's son? Once a carpenter, always a carpenter, they thought — his hands were made for woodworking, not working with sick people. Who does this carpenter with calloused hands think he is? Where did he get his healing touch?

Was it because they knew him so well that they rejected him? Knowledge can be a dangerous thing. They knew he didn't have a degree or even a certificate in the healing arts. They knew he didn't go to school to learn how to be a doctor or to the synagogue to learn to be a rabbi. He was an ordinary, homegrown son of a carpenter.

For his part, Jesus just chalks up his rejection to the old saw: "Prophets are not without honor except in their own hometown" (Luke 4: 24). Astronauts and actors; sports heroes and cartoon characters; presidents, pundits, and maybe even priests will be welcomed back to the places where they were born and raised, but not prophets.

Inner State: The Prophet's Path

On this odyssey, as we follow the map of the geography of grace to that inner safe space of the soul, we learn soon enough how the nature of prophecy — like the nature of grace itself — is frightening. The only thing the prophet can depend on is rejection. But because the vocation of the prophet is rooted deep within the very mysteries of life, the prophet isn't interested in a sign on an interstate. However, the prophet is focused on the *inner* state — the state of one's inner life that leads the prophet to speak the truth. Jeremiah, who drew a map to the sacred space we've considered in this chapter, certainly names the origin of the prophetic call: "Before I formed you in the womb, I knew you," God says to Jeremiah. "Before you were born, I dedicated you; a prophet to the nations I appointed you" (1: 4-5).

This burning sense of mission is what keeps prophets on the right track, even though they know how dangerous is the course to which they have been called. Jeremiah was afraid to accept God's call because he had seen what happened to prophets before him. His rejection was certain: He would be reviled, alienated and isolated because he allowed God's Word to consume his life. Jeremiah spoke the truth, and for speaking and living the truth he was pushed away and run out of town.

It is the same path Jesus followed. After initially praising the "appealing discourse that came from his lips," the mood of the congregation changed quickly. "Isn't this Joseph's son?" (Luke 4: 7) they asked. They began to recall that this is the carpenter's kid who grew up with their own children, who worked as an apprentice to his father and ran errands for his mother; this was the same boy who played with and went to the same schools as their own children. So they asked themselves, "Who does he think he is?"

Suddenly Jesus' message didn't sound so appealing. "They rose up and expelled him from the town" (4: 29). Indeed, the Gospel reports, they were "intending to hurl him over the edge" of a cliff, but Jesus "went straight through their midst and walked away" (4: 30).

In the geography of grace, the path of the prophet always leads to the edge, for that is where the prophet finds the people who have been pushed over the edge, who cling to the end of a rope, dangling between heaven and earth, and losing all hope. This is where the prophet finds his or her home: on the edge. Here the prophet sets up shop and seeks to live truth. But the prophet goes back and forth between the edge and the center to speak the truth, attempting to move those in the middle to the fringe so that the people who sit on the edges of our lives may become the center of our concern.

The experience of Jesus and Jeremiah is similar to that of most prophets. We can all probably name people in our own lives who have dared to speak out and, because they did, were shunned or excluded or perhaps even driven away because of the truth they spoke.

This is the bottom line, the common denominator for prophets: the truth. The truth is what Jesus spoke that day in Nazareth. The truth is what Jeremiah conveyed to his people. The truth is this: God does not exclude anyone.

Jeremiah is proclaimed as a prophet to all nations. Jesus rekindles the image of Elijah and Elisha reaching out to the outcasts. Prophets torture us with the truth — we cannot bc blind to the needs of others. We are one family in need of God and in need of each other.

Prophets call forth from us our best desires, intentions, visions and dreams. They speak God's vision that is etched upon our hearts, challenging us to reach our full potential as children of God by ridding ourselves of fear and sin and standing up in truth and in love for others. Prophets remain faithful to that which is still hidden in God's heart. And because they conform their hearts to God's will, they will necessarily be nonconformists in the eyes of the world and often in the eyes of the community.

This grace odyssey thus brings us to another moment of truth. The call of grace is to be prophetic. To live in the manner of Jesus means to confront whatever in our culture is crushing compassion, squeezing out mercy or dealing out death. The true prophet is motivated by love. People who seek to reform their business, their faith community and their world must return often to that safe, sacred space of solitude and check their bearings. Is it really love that motivates me?

And though the prophet may be bruised, broken, betrayed and pushed to the fringe for speaking the truth, the prophet can always count on God. Remember how God tells Jeremiah: "They will fight against you, but not prevail over you, for I am with you to deliver you" (1: 19). These are the words that sustain prophets in times of turmoil and trouble.

A friend once said to me that pigs and prophets are never appreciated until they are dead, until they are "cured," because while they are alive, they create such a mess. No one wants to be called a pig. And my guess is that we don't want to be called prophets either. Indeed, being prophetic means we will be misunderstood, misrepresented and maybe not missed at all. And we will not have our name etched upon a welcome sign in the town in which we were born and raised.

But if we can make our home on the edge and make friends with those who call the fringe their home, then we will be the sign that welcomes others along the most important highway of all — the highway of holiness — that leads to the very heart of God.

Psalm of the Dancing Prophet

Dancing prophet,
danger lurks in the shadows
and begins to lurch
into the light
to have the next dance.
Danger touches an emptiness
inside the prophet's soul,
a void no words
or work can fill.
Only love.
A love that is unyielding,
relentless,
starting like smoldering lust
but soon flaming
to engulf the forest
with love
that startles,
surprises,
satisfies.
Passionate winds
blow unseen in the night,
and soon the forest
is so much kindling.

Dance, prophet,
amid the raging inferno
and feel passion
burning red and hot
against the night sky.
And in the morning
the ashes will remain warm
to bare feet.

Chapter Five

Vocation as Grace:
Reflections on the One That Got Away

In each person's life there comes a time
when that one is tapped on the shoulder
and offered the opportunity to do a very special thing,
unique and fitted to that one's talent and gifts.
What a tragedy if at that moment
the person feels unprepared or unqualified for the work
which would be the person's finest hour.
—Sir Winston Churchill

I do not seek to follow
In the footsteps of the people of old;
I seek the things they sought.
—Basho

After Jesus suffered rejection in his native place, he continued his journey
to map the geography of grace. In Luke's Gospel, after holding crowds
"spellbound by his teaching" in Capernaum, performing exorcisms and
healing Simon's mother-in-law, who "was in the grip of a severe fever,"
Jesus "set out into the open country" (Luke 4: 42). But even though

Jesus knew one must make the inner journey alone, he also knew that to reform and transform the "outer space" of the world and return it to its original grace he needed company.

According to the synoptic tradition, the first four people Jesus called to follow him — Andrew, Peter, James and John — were fishermen. Considering how fishermen are known for the stories they tell about the one that got away, I wonder if there is a connection here.

But given Jesus' background, why didn't he try the carpenter union first? Certainly he could have found a few followers in the brotherhood of woodworkers and woodcarvers. In fact, since we often use the metaphor of "building community" and "building the reign of God," who would you call to build your house, a fisherman or a carpenter?

Jesus also must have had a soft spot in his heart for sheep and shepherds. In John's Gospel, he calls himself the "Good Shepherd," and there are numerous references to the "lost sheep." I've searched the Scriptures and have yet to find a reference to Jesus calling himself the "Good Fisherman." Jesus' ancestor, David, was a shepherd. Shepherds were the first ones who heard the news about Jesus' birth. They made haste to Bethlehem to see the child — and we've been following their recipe for "making haste" ever since. Jesus might have rewarded the shepherd industry by choosing representatives from this ancient profession to be his first followers.

Instead, Jesus chose four fishermen.

Going Deep: Fish or Cut Bait

Luke's account of the call of the disciples differs from other versions in the sense that Jesus almost has to prove his power to these fishermen before they'll leave their fishing business to follow him. In Matthew and Mark, Jesus is walking along the beach, sees Peter, Andrew, James and John engaged in the business of fishing and simply says, "Follow me." They drop their nets, leave their families and livelihoods, and follow Jesus on his odyssey of grace without a hint of hesitation or even a gesture of good-bye.

But Luke's account fleshes out the story a bit when Jesus shows these fishermen that he's a pretty good fisherman himself. In fact, since these professional fishermen had fished through the night without catching a thing, one might wonder why when they see Jesus' talent for finding just the right spots, they didn't say, "Hey, you're good at this! Why don't you go into business with us!" Instead, Jesus recruits the disciples to fish for people.

Several aspects of Luke's version of this familiar story may have some ramifications as we consider our own call to discipleship on this odyssey of grace. For example, Jesus convinces Peter to follow him by doing what Peter knows best. Peter is a fisherman, so to convince Peter to leave his fishing boat and "catch people" Jesus goes fishing. This seems significant considering how earlier Jesus visited Peter's house and cured Peter's mother-in-law, but Jesus' power to heal people didn't convince Peter to follow. Nor did Jesus' prowess as a teacher motivate Peter to pick up stakes and become a disciple. The story of Peter's call begins with Jesus confiscating Peter's fishing boat in order to avoid the crush of the crowd wanting to hear his words. But while Jesus is teaching the crowd, Peter and the others are "washing their nets" (Luke 5: 2). They're not listening to Jesus but are taking care of their own business.

It is only when Jesus invites them to go fishing and they catch such a large number of fish that Peter and the others drop their nets to follow him. Jesus lures Peter with the kind of bait he knows best — fishing. If we assume Jesus was a carpenter by trade and only fished recreationally, Jesus' showing these commercial fishermen that he could hold his own in their profession convinced them he was someone special.

The carpenter's desire to go fishing with the fishermen raises a second aspect that makes Luke's call of the disciples unique. Notice Jesus' invitation to Peter: "Put out into the deep water and let your nets down for a catch" (5: 4). Jesus invites Peter and the others to "go deeper" (5: 4). Peter knows better. After all, they had been fishing all night. It would be foolish to keep fishing — a waste of time.

The story suggests that when we encounter the Lord, our moment of truth has arrived. It certainly did for Peter. After fishing all night long and catching nothing — which had to leave him frustrated because this was Peter's livelihood — Jesus appears and gives him advice. At first Peter is very skeptical: "But we've been at this all night." Then he relents and goes out to deeper water. There they catch "such a great number of fish their nets were at a breaking point" (5: 6).

Peter's time has arrived. His hour has come. Here is Peter's moment of truth — or at least one of the many moments of truth he would stumble over on his odyssey of grace. When our time comes, when our moment of truth arrives to go deeper into the mystery of God's presence among us, we will soon discover — as Peter and the others did — that we are in over our heads. It's time to sink or swim, fish or cut bait. Peter knows he's in over his head after catching all the fish, so he falls to his knees and says to Jesus, "Leave me, Lord, for I am a sinful man" (5: 8).

But Jesus isn't leaving until he takes Peter and a few of his friends with him. "Do not be afraid," Jesus says. The entire grace odyssey can be summarized in those four little words: "Do not be afraid" (5: 10).

The timing of Peter's call to follow Jesus is a *kairos* moment, a moment of truth. It is, in Thomas Merton's phrase, "the time of urgent and providential decision" that changes the course of Peter's life forever. When we are faced with these *kairos* moments, how we respond will forever alter the story of our lives. We will never be the same again. This is what happens to Peter and the other disciples. They have encountered the Truth in the person of Jesus. There is no turning back to their former way of life.

The call of the first disciples in Luke's Gospel emphasizes two important qualities of the grace of vocation. First, God finds us, meets us and calls us in what we know and do best. It is in our giftedness that we hear the call of grace to discipleship. Secondly, the call to be a disciple is always about going deeper into the mystery — the paschal mystery — of God's presence among us. When we're in the middle of the mystery, it will seem like we're in over our heads.

And we are.

But remember that the one who calls us is also good at fishing. So when we think we're sinking, in over our heads, and going down for the third time, the one who says to Peter "Do not be afraid" will catch us in the net of God's love.

Peter Panned

Peter, of course, would depend often on this saving net because he would fall more than once. Peter's penchant for tripping and falling along the way or sticking his foot in his mouth at various turns on his faith odyssey is well documented. We are familiar with the stops and starts that Peter makes in the Gospels in his attempts to follow Jesus.

After boldly proclaiming that Jesus is the Messiah, he denies that Jesus should have to die and then he denies that he even knows Jesus on the night before Jesus dies. For his insight into Jesus' nature, he is awarded the keys to the kingdom. But after saying he would stand by Jesus to the very end, he drops the keys and runs away in fear. When Jesus gets up from the table and gets down on his knees to wash the feet of his disciples at the Last Supper, it is Peter who is shocked and says, "You shall never wash my feet!" (John 13: 8). Peter relents and repents only when Jesus tells him that if he doesn't let him wash his feet Peter will have no share in his heritage.

But Peter finally does get the point and is recognized not only by Jesus but also by the early Christian community as the undisputed leader of the group. Peter is the poster boy for the kind of servant leadership that comes from the depths of one's experiences — the depths of suffering where one takes up one's cross. This is where Peter receives his credentials for leadership: from his own experiences of suffering, of falling flat on his face but always relying on God's grace to help him get up again and continue the race that leads to glory.

There is no question that Jesus gave Peter a certain amount of authority after Peter has identified him as the Messiah (Matthew 16: 13-19). But it is how Peter exercises this authority that makes all the difference. Those who hold keys do wield authority and power. Jesus says as much to Peter: "Whatever you bind on earth will be bound in heaven, and whatever you loose on earth will be loosed in heaven" (16: 19). When we hold the keys of leadership, we can lock or unlock the doors. We can lock people up or lock people out. We can keep the doors open or change the locks so that even those who have keys can't get inside. We can keep people on the loose or bind them so tightly that they can never get away. Someone on the loose may be given enough rope to fashion a noose and hang out to die. And someone who is bound to the community is bound to lose — to lose one's life for Jesus' sake and the Gospel's sake: "Whoever wishes to be my follower must deny oneself, take up one's cross each day, and follow in my steps. Whoever would save one's life will lose it, and whoever loses one's life for my sake will save it" (Luke 9: 23-24).

What is this self we are asked to deny? Isn't it the "false self" that keeps us from recognizing our true self, our true nature as God's beloved children? The false self is the ego that demands recognition and affirmation to inflate itself and then becomes deflated when the perks and privileges it thinks it deserves are not forthcoming.

To get a handle on the difference between the false and the true self, we return to the image of shepherds and sheep.

From Shepherd to Sheep: Advance Scouts

It is instructive to remember that when Jesus prepared his disciples for their first missionary tour, he told them to rely on the kindness and hospitality of the people to whom they are sent. In Luke's Gospel (10: 1-12), for example, Jesus sends out seventy-two disciples as "advance scouts" to the places that he intends to visit. Scholars suggest the number 72 is important, first because it is divisible by two: Jesus sent them out in pairs because he knew discipleship is too difficult to do by oneself. More significantly, however, the number is taken from Genesis 10, where after the water retreats following the great flood there are seventy-two nations listed on the face of the earth. By appointing seventy-two disciples, Jesus implies his message is universal and will stretch to the very ends of the earth. These advance scouts were to prepare the people in the various towns and villages where Jesus would preach and teach to hear his message and believe in the good news of God's reign.

But Jesus warns these advance scouts that they will be like "lambs among wolves" (10: 3). He could easily identify with changing roles, from being shepherd to being sheep. He is both the good shepherd and the lamb of God — the one who goes out looking for the lost sheep and the one who is lost, the lamb that is slain and hung out to dry on a cross.

He tells his disciples they will not receive a standing ovation at every place they visit. Because they will be the visiting team, their field of dreams will at some times in some places become a nightmare since they will be seen not as heroes but as heretics. This may explain why few responded to Jesus' invitation: In a battle between sheep and wolves the smart money would be on the wolves to win. Jesus laments the fact that the harvest is great but the laborers are few, but by casting the disciples as "sheep among wolves" Jesus is drawing upon an ancient image. Recall how Jesus' favorite prophet, Isaiah, used this image of the lamb and wolf grazing together in perfect peace to signal the beginning of a new creation (11: 6). This is the way things were at the first creation, and Jesus' life was about restoring this sense of Shalom in bringing about the new creation.

It is this sense of peace that these advance scouts are instructed to announce when they arrive in a particular village or town. The first words from their mouths are to be these: "Peace to this house" (10: 5). As advance scouts for the reign of God, they are to announce with their lives the peace of Christ. These houses where they breathe peace would be safe places in which to tell the people the good news of salvation.

But in those places where they experience a lack of hospitality, they are to "shake the dust from their feet" (see 10: 11). Not being well received might be the reason Jesus tells his advance men and women to travel lightly. He gives very detailed instructions about what they are to take with them for the trip, and the bottom line seems to be to travel in a way that keeps them light on their feet. For example, they are not to pack in their knapsack expectations of success or concerns about failure because it will only weigh them down and stop them in their tracks. If they depend too much on their words being well-received, it may inflate their egos and tempt them to believe that they are the reason people welcome them. Or, if they are too deflated when they are not welcomed with open arms, they may lose heart and give up the journey.

By travelling lightly, these disciples will be ready and willing, open and honest enough to receive whatever people give them. If the townsfolk welcome them with open arms, they have found a safe place. If they are rejected, they simply kick the village's dust from their feet and move on.

This is an important message for us, the advance scouts of God's reign today. If we place too much emphasis on our own abilities or inability to be good news to others, then we are in danger of depending too much on applause and affirmation when we present God's message and become dejected when we are not well-received. Or we may worry so much that we are not worthy enough to proclaim God's message that we sit on our hands and close our mouths. Either way, when we are not humble enough to accept our true self, we give too much power to our false self — that "self" Jesus asks us to deny when he says, "deny your very self, take up your cross, and follow in my steps" (Matthew 16: 24).

Jesus describes our true self in the scene where the disciples return at the conclusion of Luke's "instructions for the road." The disciples return "rejoicing" because their mission has been a success. "Do not rejoice because the spirits are subjected to you," Jesus says, "but because your names are inscribed in heaven." This is our true self: We are children of a living, loving God sent to proclaim the good news of Jesus.

Those who reject us for speaking our truth actually do us a favor. After all, if we are not rejected every now and then for speaking the truth, we may just be living a lie.

Being true to the mission of grace, our shoulders will bear the imprint of heavy crosses. Our feet will know blisters and our hands will feel the sting of rejection. Our faces will be slapped more than our backs. But if we are true to the call we have received, in Paul's words, "the grace of our Lord Jesus Christ [will] be with [us]" (Galatians 6: 18).

Seeking Out the Lost: A Couple of Joes

This divine disposition to be on the lookout for the lost, the forsaken and those falling from grace might also explain why Jesus chose fishermen first. Like shepherds, fishermen were predisposed to focus their attention on the one that got away. No matter how many fish they catch, fishers will be back at the pond or the lake or the river because of the one that got away.

Is it a stretch to think that when our odyssey of grace ends, the "one that got away" will judge us?

Shepherds seek out the one that got away. Fishermen keep coming back for the one that got away. There is a message about hope in this image of fishermen. People who fish for a living must have hope. Maybe that's why Jesus chose these fishermen: He saw the hope in their eyes and the tenacity in their souls to keep going even when the odds were against them.

Paying attention to those who have been pushed aside or tossed away like human refuse and trying to bring them back reminds me of a sign I saw several years ago. New gutters were being put on the house across the street from where I was giving a retreat. The truck parked in front of the house advertised with the slogan, "Seamless Guttering." Seeing that slogan reminded me of a couple of Joes. The first is the late Joseph Cardinal Bernardin of Chicago. The second is my father.

Cardinal Bernardin came to mind when I saw the message "seamless guttering" because he often spoke and wrote about the respect and reverence we are to give to all human life, which he compared to a "seamless garment." Woven into the fabric of every human life, this garment of grace, is the belief that all life is sacred. So that's how the word "seamless" sparked a connection. But that word "guttering" also applies to Cardinal Bernardin. He was a modern-day shepherd who seemed to be on the lookout for the ones that got away, those who had fallen into the gutters of life. He so resonated not only with those he served in the Roman Catholic Church but with people throughout the world that when he died on November 14, 1996, *Newsweek* ran a cover story on his life and death.

When he discovered he was dying of cancer, he said it put his life into perspective. He said that for most of his life he was concerned with nonessentials, but when faced with a death sentence, they all faded away, allowing what is most essential to come into clear focus. When he found out he had only a few months to live, he spent most of his time with others who were dying. He fashioned a community of life out of the reality of death. Through his own experience of suffering, in his companionship with others who were facing death, Cardinal Bernardin began to see death not as an enemy but as a friend.

Because he chose to make his terminal illness and dying so public, Cardinal Bernardin stood naked before the world. He was vulnerable and open. Perhaps this vulnerability began to take root in his life in November of 1993 when he was falsely accused of abusing a seminarian while he was archbishop of Cincinnati in the 1970s. In his moment of truth Bernardin responded to the charges of sexual misconduct with "an inner strength" that he said later had to come from God alone. "For me," he wrote, "this moment of public accusation and inquiry was also a moment of grace. A moment of pain, but a moment of grace because I felt the great love and support that many people were giving me."

Within a hundred days the charges against Bernardin were proved to be groundless, and in February of 1994 the former seminarian, Steven Cook, asked a judge to drop the charges. But over the several months, the Cardinal realized that he would not be at peace with this most painful episode in his life until he met with the one who falsely accused him. "He was the sheep who had been lost," Bernardin wrote, "and, as a shepherd, I knew that I had to seek him out."

This meeting occurred on the feast of the Holy Family, December

30, 1994. Cardinal Bernardin flew to Philadelphia to meet with Steven Cook. After listening to his story and accepting his heartfelt apology, Bernardin gave Steven a Bible as a gift. Then, in the Cardinal's own words, "I took a hundred-year-old chalice out of my case. 'Steven, this is a gift from a man I don't even know. He asked me to use it to say Mass for you some day.'" With that chalice, they celebrated the Eucharist. After Mass, Bernardin had this reflection, recorded in his book *The Gift of Peace*: "In every family there are times when there is hurt, anger, or alienation. But we cannot run away from our family. We have only one family and so, after every falling out, we must make every effort to be reconciled. So, too, the church is our spiritual family. Once we become a member, we may be hurt or become alienated, but it is still our family. Since there is no other, we must work at reconciliation."

Cardinal Bernardin described that meeting with Steven Cook as the most "profound reconciliation" he had ever been part of. It was "the power of God's grace at work," he said. "It was a manifestation of God's love, forgiveness, and healing that I will never forget."

Standing before his accuser and public scrutiny, Cardinal Bernardin was as vulnerable as he had ever been in his life. That experience taught him something about being a shepherd. Steven Cook, who was dying of AIDS when he met with the Cardinal, was able to die in peace because the shepherd he had accused was willing to learn from the experience. Cardinal Bernardin was now better equipped to "seek out the lost, bring back the stray, bind up the injured."

Another Joe: A Genealogy of Grace

The second Joe who came to mind with that "seamless guttering" sign is my father. Seeing the new gutters being installed, I had a flashback to one of the least-likeable chores I had when I was a boy: cleaning the gutters. Trees surrounded the house where we lived. It was a "high" house with a steep, slanted roof in the front. Dad would hold the ladder, but one of us boys would have to climb on the roof and remove all the decaying leaves that had accumulated in the gutters during the previous fall. It was a messy job. The leaves were wet, and their smell was potent.

My dislike for this chore, however, stemmed not from the smell or the debris we would clean out from the gutters but from my fear of the height. Although I don't notice a fear of heights so much now, I certainly did then. Inching my way across the slanted roof, balance was the key. And when all the gutters were clean, climbing down from the ladder now resting at the other end of the house brought fear to the forefront. I wasn't worried that dad would let go of the ladder. I trusted him. But I didn't trust myself. Missing a step might mean losing my balance and allowing my chin to make music as I fell to the ground.

Maybe I am still afraid of heights. But high above street level is not the place where we normally look for gutters — or the people who live in them. Normally we think of gutters as things down below. Yet on this journey of grace, maybe we should be afraid of heights, especially if those heights keep us from taking the lowest place. Then, we can keep our eyes on the folks who have fallen — or been pushed — into the gutters of life, especially if they are members of our own family.

In recent years I have become more interested in my family history. When visiting Mom and Dad, I often ask about certain relatives who have passed away, how they are related, and about their lives. Every now and then if Dad isn't in the mood he'll say, "What do you want to know about them for? They never amounted to anything." Still, he's a great source of family stories: As I write this, he is about to celebrate his 80th birthday; his memory is very sharp, and he can remember people and places from when he was a small boy.

One night when I was home for supper I asked about a couple of great uncles on my dad's side of the family. They were brothers of my dad's father, and both of them died when I was relatively young. Uncle Anton, who was called "Uncle Ton," was my godfather. He died when I was five. I barely remember him. "Uncle Pete" died when I was twelve. I remember visiting the old house where he and Uncle Ton, both bachelors, lived. I recall the potbelly stove and Uncle Pete and Uncle Ton playing pinochle with my Mom and Dad.

But that's about all I remember. I can't bring to mind their features or anything about what they looked like. So I asked Dad about them — what they did for a living, what they liked and disliked, why they never married and how they died. They were poor farmers, barely scratching out a living. They loved to play cards — pinochle, mostly — and were very serious about the game. Indeed, some of the stories of the family feuds that developed over playing the wrong card have become legendary. I learned that both my uncles died of emphysema.

Neither of them made a name for himself; neither had much money when he died. They never had the slightest claim to fame. They were quiet men who kept to themselves. When they died, few people outside of the family mourned their loss. They were never wealthy, and maybe not even wise. But they lived on this earth and they left their mark, no matter how small that mark may be. Their blood runs in my veins.

Uncle Pete and Uncle Ton are part of my genealogy of grace.

It is important for us to know the names and stories of those from whom we've come, to remember and reverence the memory of those who came before us. When celebrating a birthday, for example, we celebrate more than God's gracious gift of life to one person. We celebrate how that life is passed down from one generation to the next in an ever flowing stream of redeeming grace. As Henri Nouwen wrote, "Celebrating a birthday is exalting life and being glad for it. On a birthday, we don't say, 'Thanks for what you did, or said, or accomplished.' No, we say, 'Thank you for being born and being among us.'"

As the mystic, Meister Eckhart, wrote, "Every creature is a Word of God, a book about God." As a spiritual exercise, every now and then — perhaps on a rainy day or on our birthday — it would be good to trace the genealogy of grace in our own families, in our own faces, in our own lives. It's healthy to my life of grace to dust off those books about people like my Uncle Pete and my Uncle Ton in the archives of my soul. It leads me to ask: What characteristics of their lives now influence my own? What qualities of my mother and my father do I carry with me wherever I go? Not just physical characteristics but soulful qualities that are uniquely my own?

"Celebrating a birthday," Nouwen wrote, "reminds us of the goodness of life, and in this spirit we really need to celebrate people's birthdays every day, by showing gratitude, kindness, forgiveness, gentleness, and affection. These are ways of saying: 'It is good that you are alive; it's good that you are walking with me on this earth.'"

A Sheepish Look and Plenty of Fish

Someone once described the spiritual journey as "continually falling on your face, getting up, brushing yourself off, looking sheepishly at God, and taking another step." That seems to summarize pretty well the journey of discipleship in the state of grace.

I suspect that the phrase, "looking sheepish" comes from the look on the face of lost sheep. We've seen the look on our own faces. It's a look of embarrassment when we become aware of a fault or mistake. It's the look I had on my face when I was a child and an hour before supper, when Mom wasn't looking, I would take a cookie from the cookie jar. When Mom came back into the kitchen, she could read the look on my face. It was a "sheepish" look, a guilty look. She knew right away that something was "fishy," even if we were having meatloaf for supper.

If we have ever experienced being lost and needing to stop and ask for directions — especially if we were so sure of where we were going when we started — we know this look. If we've ever been told by others to "get lost," we know another kind of sheepish look — the look of shame and pain. But this sheepish look will not last for long. Once it dawns on the lost sheep that she has been found, a smile fills her face. Now the look is one of love. Now the face of shame has a new name: joyful. Full of joy.

If we have ever been found by another, or finally found the place where we were going after hours of being lost, then we also know the look of joy on the face of the sheep after he has been found. Or the look on the face of the woman who found the lost coin after turning her house upside down.

When we're feeling small, God's love is large. When we're feeling lost, God will find us. When we have that sheepish look on our faces for what we've done or what we've failed to do, God will give our faces a lift. And the lift that will turn our faces from sheepish looks to joyful looks is the grace of forgiveness as we recognize the presence of pardon and peace.

Certainly Peter and the other disciples had to have a sheepish look on their faces that day Jesus appeared to them on the beach after his resurrection (John 21). After all, when he needed them most, they had run away. When the Lamb of God was led to the slaughter, Peter and the others had been like scared sheep that scattered.

Two familiar proverbs come to mind when reflecting on this story that is commonly referred to as the "Breakfast on the Beach" when Jesus appears to his disciples at the Sea of Tiberias. The first is often used to comfort someone who has been dumped by a boyfriend or girlfriend: "There are plenty of fish in the sea."

This is what Jesus says to the disciples after they fished all night but didn't catch a thing: "There are plenty of fish in the sea." On a literal level, he was right, of course. As the last chapter of John's Gospel says, after Jesus' suggestion to cast their net "off to the starboard side," the disciples "took so many fish that they could not haul the net in" (21: 6).

Beyond the literal level, however, that ancient proverb, "There are plenty of fish in the sea" may also bring some symmetry to the call of the disciples. Remember how when Jesus first called Peter and Andrew and James and John, they were doing what they are doing in this Gospel scene: fishing. At the core of their identity, they were fishermen. When Jesus called them to follow him the first time, he used this as a metaphor: "I will make you fishers of men and women."

In the light of the resurrection, the proverb "There are plenty of fish in the sea" reflects the disciples' new challenge. When Peter "went aboard and hauled ashore the net loaded with sizable fish — one hundred and fifty-three of them" (John 21: 11) — the initial invitation for these fishermen to follow Jesus now takes on enormous possibilities and remarkable responsibilities. They will no longer be fishing for a few folks at the local watering hole or putting out a line down by the river. Because of the resurrection of Jesus, the number of fish they catch in the saving net of God's grace and love will be more than they dare imagine. Now salvation will reach the ends of the earth. Now they will cast their nets far and wide to include as many people as possible. And "in spite of the great number, the net was not torn" (21: 11).

We will know where we are going on this odyssey of grace when we keep our minds and hearts open so that no one is left out or slips through the net out of sight and out of mind.

Found at Sea: Finders Keepers

The second familiar proverb that comes to mind in relation to the story of the miraculous catch on the sea of Tiberias is "Finders keepers, losers weepers." Now, while the notion of this proverb is childish and ethically ambiguous, in light of the resurrection narratives — and particularly the role Simon Peter plays in these stories — the old saying might give us some new meaning.

Peter thinks he's found a real keeper in Jesus when he leaves his nets, his livelihood and his family to follow him. But after Peter betrays his teacher and friend by denying him and running away when Jesus needed him most, Peter thinks he has lost everything. After denying Jesus, he weeps bitterly. "Finders keepers, losers weepers."

Still uncertain about the events that occurred after the resurrection, Peter is trying to make some sense out of it all. So he goes back to a familiar spot to do something that is second nature to him: fishing. It is fitting that Peter and the others are fishing on the Sea of Tiberias when Jesus appears to them the third time "after being raised from the dead" (John 21: 4). It fits not only because this is what at least four of them were doing when Jesus called them the first time, but because, after all that happened, they are "lost at sea." They are feeling lost and forsaken. They're trying to find an anchor in a swirling sea of confusion and doubt.

Besides "Breakfast on the Beach," we might also call this appearance of Jesus after the resurrection, "Found at Sea." Peter and the disciples are no longer losers and weepers. Jesus has found them. And you know what they say: "Finders keepers." Unlike the countless fish these fishermen threw back into the sea in their prior profession because the fish they caught were too small, Jesus the fisherman knows that even with all their mistakes and missed opportunities Peter and the others are "keepers." He won't be throwing them back to their former way of life.

Our faith odyssey presents us with these two important truths found in ancient proverbs: "There are plenty of fish in the sea" and "Finders keepers, losers weepers." There are plenty of fish in the sea, so we never need feel alone. And when we feel like we're lost at sea and drowning in our tears, remember that God always keeps what God has found. We won't be thrown back because we are too small or too weak or too old. It's God's rule of fishing: "Finders keepers."

This is grace: to realize that God has found us. No matter how often we run and hide or lose our way or get lost in the dark, God will continue to find us. When we embrace the grace of this vocation, we do what Jesus did for the disciples that day on the beach, and what the disciples did after being found. This is our identity as ministers of grace, as minstrels of the dawn of a new creation: to provide a place where the lost can be found, where those who have strayed can be brought back to the table, where those who are injured can bind their wounds.

As minstrels of the dawn of this new creation where all will be welcome, all will find a place and all will be one, we are willing to enter the darkness caused by missed opportunities and preoccupations and to be occupied only with the God we meet in the other. When we have the courage to do this, all the nonessentials fade away or at least are seen in their proper perspective. When we sit or stand or kneel before this awesome mystery of God's divine presence we see in the one who got away, we are in touch at last with what is essential.

And what is essential is seeing the presence of God, the presence of Christ, in every person we meet along the way.

Psalm of the Minstrels of the Dawn

Compassionate Creator,
like a shepherd, you seek out the lost,
you bring back those who have strayed or been betrayed,
you bind up the wounds of those who are injured.

You anointed your Son, Jesus Christ,
as the incarnation of your compassion in our world.
He is the eternal priest and kin to all of creation.
As priest, he offered his life on the altar of the cross
and redeemed the human race.
As our kin, he is our brother
who claims sovereignty over all creation,
that he may present to you, Creator of all,
an eternal and universal kindom:
a kindom of truth and love,
a kindom of holiness and hopefulness,
a kindom of justice and mercy,
of grace and peace.

With all the prophets and sages of ages past,
lovers and dreamers of this kindom of peace abiding on the earth,
with all creatures and all of creation,
we affirm our commitment
to see you and to serve you in one another.
With the help of your grace
May we always be ministers of your mercy
And minstrels for the dawn of a new creation.

Chapter Six

Overshadowed by Grace:
When Night Turns into Day

Perhaps all the dragons in our lives
Are princesses who are only waiting to see us act, just once,
With beauty and courage.
Perhaps everything that frightens us is,
In its deepest essence,
Something helpless that wants our love.
—Rainer Maria Rilke

All alone and feeling blue,
There's no one to tell my troubles to.
Me and my shadow,
Strolling down the avenue.
—Billy Rose

As we reflected in the last chapter, finding our true self involves taking up our cross. Indeed, on this odyssey of faith we find our footing under the shadow of the cross, and the cross casts a long and powerful shadow on this journey of faith. As we follow this map through a land of grace, in this chapter we take a closer look at the shadow side of life and see what it has to teach us and tell us about grace.

The shadow is an important symbol in a reflection on grace. Some might suggest the shadow represents the antithesis of grace. If one thinks of grace as light, shadows would reflect only darkness. If grace is the dawn and we are minstrels of the dawn, then even though shadows are created by light they seem to be more reflective of the night. And that would make us night stalkers, children of the night.

But in the language of the soul, the shadow plays a pivotal role. Primitive traditions believed that the shadow represented the "alter ego" and, particularly, reflected the spirits of those who have died. If this is the case, then shadows verify that a person is real — a "real presence." A person who creates a shadow truly exists. Therefore, the real presence of Jesus suggests he must have cast a shadow. Jesus was a real person. The one we call the "light of the world" cast the longest shadow the world has ever seen.

Some might balk at this suggestion since we sometimes think of a person's shadow as one's sin — as in the idea that people who do deeds in darkness would not do these same deeds in the light of day. But in psychological circles, though a person's shadow side may represent one's selfish side, it need not reflect moral overtones. Rather, the shadow may represent that which is hidden from view but is still very real. It may call forth a person's intuitive nature. When we say we have an intuition about something, we can't put our finger on it but believe it is true because we have a certain feeling about it.

Shadows play on the landscape of our soul, sometimes scaring us half to death, inviting us to consider something about ourselves that may be hidden from view but may hold a truth or a gift that will give our life meaning. Perhaps shadows are like the dragons Rainer Maria Rilke speaks of in *Letters to a Young Poet*; perhaps they are really "princesses who are only waiting to see us act, just once, with beauty and courage."

However we perceive our shadow that accompanies us as we "stroll down the avenue," it will provide us with many moments of truth.

Overshadowed by Grace

In the Christian story, one of those prime moments of truth happened to a humble young maiden who lived in Nazareth. Recall that when the angel appears to Mary and announces to her that she would be the mother of Jesus, Mary asks the angel, "How can this be?" The angel says to her, "The Holy Spirit will come upon you, and the power of the Most High will overshadow you; therefore, the child to be born will be called holy, the Son of God" (Luke 1: 35).

In the language of grace, our shadows can be overwhelmed by the power of God's presence. We call this being "overshadowed." This is how Mary becomes "full of grace" — the power of the Most High overshadows her. This is how we receive the fullness of grace — when we allow the power of the Most High to overwhelm us. When our shadow sides are "overshadowed" by the power of God's grace, we see the face of God.

What does Mary see that day in Nazareth when the angel Gabriel appears to her? How does she react to this experience of being overshadowed by God's grace? First of all, remember that Gabriel greets her with the words, "Hail, O favored one, God is with you!" (1: 28). Mary is already "full of grace" — that is what being called "favored one" means. In the Hebrew Scriptures, to be favored by God is to be full of grace.

But soon Mary finds out that she would be receiving the "fullness of grace." And her reaction to that angel's greeting, according to Luke, is to be "deeply troubled" (1: 29). That's the trouble with angels: They come out of nowhere and scare us half to death. Seeing that Mary is frightened, Gabriel says to her, "Do not be afraid, Mary, for you have found favor with God" (1: 30). Then the angel proceeds to tell her the news that she is going to have a baby! Not just any baby, but the one who "will be called the Son of the Most High" (1: 32).

That is when Mary raises the practical issue of "How?" Notice that Mary doesn't ask, "Why?" I suspect that would be the first question many of us would ask under these circumstances. An angel appearing out of the blue would prompt us to ask, "Why me?" That question was already answered, though, when the angel greets Mary by calling her the favored one. She did nothing to deserve this divine visitation. It is because of God's favor to her that Mary is chosen. The same is true for us: When we are chosen by God to do some important work for the advancement of God's reign, we might ask, "Why me?" But the question is moot. We did nothing to deserve the call. It is God's grace, God's favor, that chooses us.

Mary also doesn't ask for a timetable. In her conversation with the angel, she doesn't ask, "When? When will this happen?" Mary doesn't seem to be interested in God's timing in all of this or whether this invitation to be the mother of Jesus will fit into her schedule. She doesn't look at her calendar and say to the angel, "Oh, sorry, having a baby now just doesn't fit in to my future plans. Listen, why don't you come back at another time — when I'm older and more established in my career. Then we can talk about having a baby."

No, it is not a matter of timing that concerns Mary. It is the practical matter of how all this will take place since she and her fiancé Joseph have not been sleeping together. Mary's mother, Anne, has certainly given her "the lecture" we commonly refer to as "the birds and the bees." Mary is not naïve. She knows the score. She wants to know more: "How shall this be, since I have no husband?" (1: 34).

Mary raises the issue. She takes the obvious and honest question out of the shadows of her own soul and asks the angel how. But her question is overshadowed by the power of God's grace as the angel tells her, "the power of the Most High will overshadow you" (1: 35).

The angel's visit to Mary and the power of life that overshadowed her reminds me of a time when I was visiting a close friend over the Christmas holidays. Early one morning during my prayer time I was writing in my journal when I noticed the miniature evergreen in the living room. As I looked for a symbol to focus my meditation, I found two of them. First I noticed hanging on one of the delicate branches of this evergreen an outline of an angel. It was an angel ornament made from the thinnest of wire. It hung almost unnoticed near the top of the tree. Its wiry hands were folded, and hanging from its hands was a heart — like those heart-shaped mints one gives on Valentine's Day. Also resting in the arms of that tree was a small nest. In these two symbols — an angel and a nest — I found rest for my soul.

On this faith odyssey, we need those people and those places where we can rest. We need those times when the world seems outlined with angels and these angels have hearts to hold. What could be the point of an angelic visitation, of divine intervention, if there is not a heart to hold? We need to find rest now and then in the arms of a good friend, a spouse, a sister or brother, a mother, father or other angel.

I remember in grade school the sisters used to tell us to scoot over and leave room on our seats for our guardian angels. They also told us to sit still — which was then, is now, and always will be a good way to pray. When we scoot over and sit still, we may just find we are not alone.

In one of his poems, the Sufi mystic Rumi wrote, "Birds make great sky-circles of their freedom. How do they learn it? They fall, and falling, they're given wings."

When we think we're falling from grace, we are given wings — the wings of faith that will hold us up and lift us free. These wings — found in the arms of a friend or in the embrace of a sacred space that holds us for a while — will help us catch our breath and rest until grace overshadows us.

The world is indeed outlined by angels. So scoot over and make some room. Then sit still, open your eyes, and see your shadow.

Getting Out of the Way

As Mary shows us, when we are "full of grace" we are "empty of self." In order to be a channel of God's grace, we need to get out of the way.

Once upon a time there was a woman who lived such a godly life that even the angels rejoiced at the sight of her. Yet in spite of her goodness, she had no idea that she was holy. She just went about her routine tasks, distributing kindness and goodness the way a flower might spread its fragrance or a candle might lend its light to a room.

Her holiness was found in her ability to forget each person's past and to look at the person right in the present. She looked beyond each one's appearance to the very core of each one's heart. She saw beneath the scars of self-inflicted sins to the child that was within. This is how she loved and forgave everyone she met. She saw nothing extraordinary about this. It was simply the way she looked at people and the way she saw the world. Some would suggest to her that she take off her rose-colored glasses to see people and the world as they truly are. But she would smile and say, "I don't wear glasses."

One day, an angel appeared to her and said, "I have been sent by God to give you anything you wish. Just ask and God will deliver it. So, what would you like? Would you want, for example, the gift of healing?"

"Oh no," said the woman, "I think I'd rather leave the healing to God."

"Well, then," the angel said, "would you want to bring sinners back to the path of holiness?"

The woman smiled and said to the angel, "It's not for me to touch human hearts. That's your job."

"Good point," the angel said. "So, how would you like to be such a model of holiness that people will be drawn to imitate you?"

The woman blushed and said, "I prefer not to be the center of attention."

The angel was becoming frustrated. "What then? What do you wish for?"

"I wish only for the grace of God," the woman said. "The grace of God — that is all I desire."

"No," the angel said. "You must ask for a miracle or else God will force one upon you."

"Well, in that case, I shall ask for this: Let good be done through me, but don't let me be aware of it."

So the angel granted the woman's request. The woman's shadow was endowed with such extraordinary healing power that whenever or wherever her shadow fell, so long as she had her back to it, amazing things happened. The sick were healed, the land was productive, the backs of those weighed down by sorrow and grief grew straight again, the eyes of the lost staring into space focused on love again and the blank faces of those in despair were colored with hope again.

But because this woman had her back turned to all of this, she knew nothing of the power of her shadow. Indeed, everyone's attention was so focused on the shadow that they forgot about the woman.

And so her wish that good be done through her without her knowing it was fulfilled.

Being Overshadowed: Sibling Rivalry

But there is another kind of overshadowing that can occur in life that may leave us empty of grace because we are full of ourselves.

Sometimes in life we are overshadowed not by the presence of God but by another person. In a competitive world, this is rather common. It is not unusual for one person to overshadow another in sports or politics or business or even religion. A charismatic leader will cast a large shadow so that whoever succeeds him or her will likely have to wrestle in the shadows of the predecessor's success before he or she enjoys the spotlight.

Sometimes this experience of being "overshadowed" by another occurs in families, among siblings. Consider the story in the Book of Numbers (Chapter 12) involving an ancient case of sibling rivalry among Moses, Miriam and Aaron.

Miriam is having a tough day and has stretched herself out on the couch to complain and perhaps draw some pity from her family. She moans to her brothers Moses and Aaron, "Nobody loves me! The whole world hates me!"

Without skipping a beat her brother Aaron says, "That's not true, Miriam. Some people don't even know you."

Granted, that exchange sounds more like something Lucy would say to Linus in a *Peanuts* cartoon than something out of Scripture, but a discourse similar to this occurs in Chapter 12 of the Book of Numbers. According to the story, both Miriam and Aaron are having a rough day. Their "pity pot" is boiling because they feel their brother Moses is getting entirely too much attention. Moses is receiving all the headlines, while they are relegated to footnotes. As sometimes happens in families, offices, communities of faith and other settings, Miriam and Aaron complain because Moses is enjoying the spotlight while they are suffering in the shadows. On the face of it, this sibling rivalry starts because Miriam and Aaron are upset that Moses has married a foreigner. But beneath the surface their complaint is that Moses gets all the credit, all the glory. They want their due. After all, they are important people too.

Both Miriam and Aaron have the credentials and a long list of accomplishments to warrant attention. After all, Miriam is called a "prophetess" (Exodus 15: 30), and Aaron is Moses' "right hand man" in that story about the Israelites achieving victory in an important battle so long as Moses can keep his hands raised up to the heavens (Exodus 17: 8-13). So both Miriam and Aaron can make a case for their important place in God's plan of salvation.

When this happens in community or business or on a parish staff, a meeting is called to clear the air. When one member of the family is seen as a favorite or one employee seems to have the inside track to the boss, feelings get ruffled. In the case of Moses, Miriam and Aaron, the boss does call a meeting. "Come out, you three, to the tent of meeting," God says (Numbers 12: 4).

Well, the air was anything but clear as God appears to them "in a pillar of cloud" (12: 5). God calls Aaron and Miriam to step forward, and God explains the situation to them in no uncertain terms. "Look," God says, "when there are prophets among you, I will make myself known to them in visions and dreams. But Moses is more than a prophet. I have entrusted to Moses my whole house. Moses needs to know what's on my mind, what the divine plan is, and that is why I speak to Moses face to face, clearly, and not in riddles. That is why Moses sees me as I am" (see 12: 6-8).

It is clear from this passage that the cloud that overshadows Moses, Miriam and Aaron is a storm cloud. God is angry with Miriam and Aaron because of their whining and complaining. "Why," God asks them, "were you not afraid to speak against my servant Moses?" This storm cloud rumbles with thunder, and then lightning strikes. Miriam is stricken with leprosy. After the divine storm cloud passes, Aaron sees what has happened to his sister Miriam and pleads with Moses, "Do not punish us for a sin we have so foolishly committed" (12: 11).

Moses' reaction to this striking turn of events shows what a charismatic leader he truly is. He is described in this passage as a humble man, the only one on the face of the earth to visit with God "face-to-face" and live. It recalls Moses' first meeting with God on the mountain when he was tending his father-in-law's flock and God appears to him in the burning bush. Moses hid his face then because he knew no one could look at God's face and live. But now the relationship between God and Moses is so close, so intimate, that Moses could not only look God in the eye but could speak to God directly and live.

Yet Moses' humility always reminds him of his place. Though God has given him this incredible gift of being able to speak to the Divine One face-to-face, Moses knows his place; he knows he is nothing without God. Moses' siblings, Miriam and Aaron, have not yet learned to be humble. It was their pride that got them into trouble in the first place. They were proud of their accomplishments, and they wanted God to recognize them for the outstanding contributions they were making to God's cause. Still, Aaron and Miriam are not "too proud to beg" when their pride gets the best of them and the worst from God.

When God turns Miriam into a leper, Aaron pleads with Moses to talk to God on behalf of their sister. Moses, the humble man that he is, does not hold a grudge against his brother and sister for speaking behind his back. Instead, with graciousness he turns to God and prays, "Heal her, O God, I beseech thee" (12: 13).

Each of us every now and then climbs into the pity pot and turns up the heat because we don't feel we get the credit we deserve or the recognition we desire. But true humility, as exemplified by Moses in this scene with his siblings, and by Mary when the angel announces to her the astonishing news that she would be the mother of Jesus, means knowing that all we are and all that we have comes from God's gracious heart. When we acknowledge this truth, we will not be envious of another's accomplishments; we will not be jealous of another's gifted position.

When we are overshadowed by grace, it will be difficult at times to know our place. We need to trust that God will help us find that place. God only asks that we remain humble and grateful for whatever role we are given in the Divine One's unfolding plan of salvation. Such a humble stance will serve us well, will help us to live gracefully, especially when the storm clouds of hate and fear hover around us and threaten to overwhelm us. Unlike the story of Moses, Miriam and Aaron when the funnel clouds of fury were fueled by God's wrath, some storm clouds contain jealousy, pride and prejudice. These are the shadows of sin. To reflect on shadows of evil, we need to go back to the beginning.

Into the Shadows: The Face of Evil

In the face of evil it is God's grace that will ultimately triumph. In one sense, the story of Adam and Eve is a story about knowledge being a dangerous thing. The story says that Adam and Eve did not take God's commission at face value: They wanted to know more. When they listened to the spirit of evil — a fallen angel disguised as a serpent, as the story goes — rather than trusting in God's grace, they knew too much. They knew more than they wanted to know.

They discovered they were naked. This didn't bother them before; indeed, they rejoiced in the beauty of their bodies made in God's image. But believing in the serpent's promise that "knowledge is power" instead of God's promise that "truth is power" and "truth will set you free," Adam and Eve bit off more than they could chew. They found the knowledge they gained hard to swallow. God only wanted to protect them. God only wanted them to enjoy each other and all creation. Instead, they chose pride over protection. They chose death over everlasting life. They chose knowledge over trust.

Somehow God had to reverse this trend without denying the freedom of choice. So God chose a poor handmaid, a peasant girl, and claimed her "full of grace." Mary could have asked to know more when this angel fell from the sky and appeared on her porch. She could have asked a thousand questions but she only had one — "How can this be?"

God's question to Adam and Eve is about location: "Where are you?" (Genesis 3: 9). In business, location is everything. In spirituality, it is equally true: "Where are we?" God will find us wherever we are — as God found Mary. But we will remain lost in the clouds, overshadowed by evil instead of grace, if we remain infatuated with original sin — pride over protection — rather than embracing the original grace: "God is with you!"

In the doctrine of the Immaculate Conception, Roman Catholics believe Mary was "full of grace" from the moment of her conception. How can this be? If we have to ask because we want to know more — after all, knowledge is power — the answer is found in the angel's words to Mary: "Nothing is impossible with God."

But this is not the question. "How?" asks for specifics, for details, for facts. Mary asked "how," but the answer she received is like the one we used to get when we raised our hands in second grade and asked Sister to explain the Trinity: "It's a mystery." The angel says to Mary that "the Holy Spirit will come upon you and the power of the Most High will overshadow you."

Right. That explains it.

Maybe it does. Adam and Eve tried to escape the shadow of the Divine One. They wanted to know everything, and so even though the power of the Most High had created them and overshadowed them with abundant life, Adam and Eve escaped the shadow of the divine arm. Once they ran from God's shadow, they saw they were naked. In their shadow they saw shame and blame.

In our quest for knowledge and power, we've been running from our shadow ever since.

Of course, not all knowledge is bad. Nor is the quest for knowledge an evil course. If we trace the roots of the tree of knowledge, we discover it is the tree of good and evil. Eve became the mother of all humans, the story says. Life is good. But just as no mother or father can look out for their children all the time — at some point in the growing process parents have to let go, children have to choose — so the choices presented to Adam and Eve are also presented to each of us, their children. We can gain the knowledge to alleviate the pain of others — as we have seen so often with scientific and medical discoveries that cure illnesses. Or we can try to attain knowledge to gain the upper hand in the race to nowhere — as we saw in the nuclear arms race.

When we are surrounded by shadows, the choice is ours. We can humbly accept being overshadowed by God's grace or escape God's shadow and try to make it on our own. But as our faith story suggests, when we try to escape the shadow of God's arm, we ultimately fail and soon find ourselves standing in a familiar place: under the shadow of the cross.

The Shadow Knows: Mary's Sixth Sense

There are numerous shadow stories — of people coming out of the shadows — in the passion account of Jesus. Each of these stories shines a light on an aspect of faith, helping to form the soul in this odyssey of grace. One of my favorites is Jesus' visit to the home of three of his friends — Mary, Martha and Lazarus (John 12: 1-9). By John's account, Jesus was arrested because he raised Lazarus from the dead. So it may surprise us that, with the authorities hot on his heels, Jesus would go to the scene of the crime for which he would be arrested. His crime, of course, was causing a public nuisance, disturbing the peace (defined as the status quo) by bringing someone who was dead back to life.

Yet Jesus attends a dinner given for him by his three good friends. What was the reason for this celebration? Instead of a funeral dinner for Lazarus, this was a celebration of life. The Gospel says Lazarus was with Jesus at the table. In fact, the Gospel also says that the chief priests planned to kill Lazarus too because so many people were believing in Jesus on account of Lazarus.

This raises the question, "How many people come to believe on account of me?" Was Lazarus giving witness or was simply sitting at the table with the one who raised him from the dead witness enough?

I can imagine Jesus and Lazarus talking about that day in Bethany when Jesus called his name and Lazarus came shuffling out of the tomb. One of those at the table — Peter, maybe, since he was often the one to ask the most questions — asks Lazarus, "What was it like? What was it like to be buried for more than four days? Did you feel anything? Did you see anything — like the proverbial light at the end of the tunnel — or in your case, at the end of the tomb? Tell us, Lazarus, what was it like to be dead?"

Jesus puts his finger to his lips as if to tell Peter to keep his mouth shut and his questions to himself because he knows his friend Lazarus has had to answer the same questions over and over since the event happened. But Lazarus pours Peter some more wine and tries to explain. "I wasn't in a coma, Pete," Lazarus says. "I was dead. Literally, clinically dead. No pulse. No brain waves. Nothing. So I don't remember a thing. I had bought the farm, cashed in my chips, kicked the bucket. Whatever cliché you want to use, I was dead. And now I'm alive!"

"Go figure," Peter says.

And that's exactly what the chief priests were doing. They were figuring that many would come to believe in Jesus on account of Lazarus. He had to die again. But this time, he would have to stay dead. So Jesus must die, or his friends — like Lazarus — would live forever.

As Jesus and Lazarus and some of the other disciples continue to talk about that day, Martha is in the kitchen getting supper ready. Mary has set the table, but since it would be a while before supper, she brings a jar of oil into the room. Silence falls over the room as Mary approaches Jesus. She kneels before him and gently pours the oil over his feet. It is a gesture of hospitality, a sacrament of welcome or maybe of gratitude — remember that Mary, Martha and Lazarus are overflowing with gratitude for what Jesus has done for them.

But in thinking about this scene, maybe Mary didn't anoint Jesus as a ritual of gratitude or hospitality. Maybe Mary had a sixth sense.

Mary and all the others who had gathered to mourn Lazarus after he died saw a dead man walking when he came out of the tomb at Jesus' invitation. Now *Jesus* would be the "dead man walking." He was on death row. Mary and the others didn't know it, but Jesus did. That is why when Judas complained about the waste — especially since he was counting the money but not counting the cost of discipleship — Jesus told him to leave her alone. Jesus knew his execution date had been set even before he was arrested. He knew this was the anointing of one who is about to die.

The Shadow Smells: The Odor of Arrogance

The fragrance of the perfume with which Mary anointed the body of Jesus filled the house that night in Bethany. By the end of the week, however, another odor would take over the whole city of Jerusalem: the smell of death.

One of the fragrances in Calvin Klein's signature line of perfumes is called "Obsession." I think the odor we identify with one of the main characters in the passion story might be called "Arrogance." Yes, let's call this new odor "Arrogance by Pontius Pilate." This is his signature line: "What is truth?" He asks this of Jesus as he interrogates him (John 18: 38), trying to find some reason not to charge him with treason.

But Pilate doesn't wait for an answer. The Truth is staring him in the face, but Pilate turns away. Yet maybe it does make a difference when the Truth is present, when the Truth has spoken. Perhaps the Truth that sets one free can make a dent, because Pilate goes to the crowd and says, "I find no crime in him" (18: 38).

Pilate, however, is an arrogant man. He has to show he's in charge. He's willing to release a prisoner and anticipates that he will free the Truth. Instead, because the Lie has become so pervasive, the crowd shouts for more lies to be released. Keep the Truth locked up, they scream. Give us Barabbas!

What is that smell? A skunk? A dead animal? No, it's arrogance. A new fragrance — or, shall we say, odor — by Pontius Pilate. He will save face by having the Truth crucified.

Pilate is given a large role and many lines in John's passion account. There is a sense he wants Jesus to go free. But the scent is unmistakable: The smell of fear leads to death. "Pilate," John writes, "became even more afraid, and went back into the praetorium and said to Jesus, 'Where are you from?'" (John 19: 9).

Jesus remains silent. This silence releases Pilate's pungent perfume. "Do you not speak to me? Do you not know that I have the power to release you and I have the power to crucify you?" (19: 10).

When we have to tell others what kind of power we have, we have already relinquished whatever power we possess. When we have to remind others who is in charge, we have lost all authority. Jesus smells a rat. He says, "You would have no power over me if it had not been given to you from above." But then Jesus releases this dead rat from the trap of Pilate's own making as he says, "For this reason the one who handed me over to you has the greater sin" (19: 11). This must make Pilate smell as fresh and clean as a spring morning because once again he wants to free the Truth. He still doesn't realize it is the other way around: The Truth will set us free.

In the end, though, Pilate comes across smelling of death. He doesn't wash his hands of this crime in John's account, but his fragrance of arrogance is evident in the end. When people complain about the inscription Pilate had written and placed on the cross, "The King of the Jews," Pilate, with his nose in the air, says, "What I have written, I have written" (John 19: 21-22).

Remember what the people said when Jesus told them to roll away the stone at Lazarus' grave? "It has been four days, there will be a stench" (John 11: 39). Death smells. There is no way around it. Death stinks. There is no fragrance that will cover the smell. No air freshener will hide the odor. Nicodemus tries. After asking Pilate for Jesus' body, he brings "a mixture of myrrh and aloes weighing about one hundred pounds" (John 14: 39) to the grave to anoint the body of Jesus. A hundred pounds of perfume and spices to anoint the body of Christ!

But the smell of death will linger. There is a stench: the foul odor of betrayal, the fragrance of arrogance, the smell of death. Three days in the tomb — not as long as Lazarus, but long enough. Yes, there is a stench. Do Peter and John smell it the morning Mary tells them the tomb is empty? Is that why John who arrives in the tomb first, waits for the slower, older Peter to go first: Is he afraid of what he might smell?

Or is his sense of smell still stuffed up by his failure to stop Judas when he sniffed the odor of betrayal on the night before Jesus died?

Under the Shadow of the Cross: John's Silence

One final shadow story from the passion account occurs at the Last Supper Jesus has with his friends. In John's version of the story, after Jesus announces that the one who will betray him is at the table, Peter motions to John to ask Jesus, "Who is it?" (John 13: 25). John leans close to Jesus' chest and learns it is Judas. Jesus identifies his betrayer as "the one to whom I give the morsel of bread" (13: 26). The others at the table do not hear what Jesus tells John. But John sees who Jesus gives the morsel of bread to.

The Gospel suggests that John keeps the identity of the betrayer to himself. He doesn't tell Peter or the other disciples that Judas is the one who is about to hand Jesus over to the authorities. When Jesus tells Judas to "hurry up in what you are about to do" (13: 27), the others think Jesus is telling Judas to see about the preparations for Passover or maybe to give money to the poor since he held the common purse. (Remember how upset Judas was a few days before when Mary used all that oil to anoint the body of Jesus.)

Why didn't John, who knew what Judas was about to do, try to stop him? Why didn't he call out to the others, "Stop him at the door! He's going to betray the rabbi! He's the one!" Or, if John didn't want to create a scene, why didn't he get up from the table himself while Judas was leaving and try to reason with him one-on-one? Why didn't John try to convince Judas to change his mind, change his course of action? He knew what Judas was about to do. Why didn't the beloved disciple try to stop the betrayer? Can we hold John accountable for what he failed to do?

Maybe it was all too confusing to John. He was young. He was afraid. He didn't know what to do. The whole night was just a blur. It got off to such an upsetting start when Jesus washed the feet of his disciples instead of allowing the servants to do it. He might as well have turned over the tables. Well, in a sense, that's exactly what Jesus did: He turned the tables. "The last shall be first and the first shall be last" (Matthew 19: 30). "As I have done, so you must do" (John 13: 15). John's head must have been spinning with all the wine and washing of feet and stories about their ancestors eating in haste with their loins girt and their sandals on their feet.

It was all too much. And then Jesus said that one of his closest friends would betray him. John knew who it wasn't. He knew he would never betray Jesus. Even though Peter insisted that he ask Jesus to identify the scoundrel who would turn him in, John never told Peter.

And he never stopped Judas from doing what he did.

The evening was moving like the great story said their forebears did that night so long ago when they were in flight — or maybe fright. Although the sight of blood on the porch was absent that night, the sight of blood in the cups was frightening enough for John. That's what Jesus told them as he passed the cup of wine around: "This is my blood, the blood of the new and everlasting covenant" (Luke 12: 20). With all these ancient rituals taking on new meaning, can we blame John for not speaking up and stopping Judas from doing his misdeed?

Yes, there was much to scare John half to death that night. But Judas made sure that by the next afternoon those who were frightened half to death would be taken the rest of the way.

John was afraid. But he found his courage later under the shadow of the cross. When everyone else ran away, John stayed. And he heard his friend say, "Here is your mother." And to his mother, the rabbi said, "Here is your son" (John 19: 26-27). John found his future under the shadow of the cross. Like the woman who gave birth to his friend and whom he would now welcome into his home as his own mother, John was "overshadowed by grace."

Psalm of Me and My Shadow

Where can I run from your call?
Where can I hide from your presence?
Wherever I go, you are there
to open a window
and look inside my soul.

Life seems so long when one is lonely.
Too short when one is busy.
Too loud when one is searching.
Too quiet when one is listening.

I stand at the crossroads
and wonder which way I shall go.
Either way I run,
you will be there.

It matters not which way I decide.
You only say, "Don't look back."
I check the map.
I have been here before.

Familiar as it seems, I am not lost.
No, I know where I want to go.
It's how to get there
that becomes my prayer.

Chapter Seven

Saving Grace: When Time Goes By, Slowly

Don't turn your head.
Keep looking at the bandaged place.
That's where the light enters you.
And don't believe for a moment that you're healing yourself.
—Rumi

When we stand under the shadow of our own crosses and losses, time stands with us and is very still.

Time stands still.

What they say about time flying when we're having fun is true. But the opposite is also true: When we're in pain or suffering or grieving, the minutes seem to struggle by. Time crawls, it doesn't fly when we are suffering.

Suffering can make us more compassionate or more cantankerous. It can make us bitter or it can make us better. Every experience begs the same question: What did I learn? What did this experience teach me?

As we trace our own experiences of suffering and loss, what have we learned from these experiences? How have we been changed by what we've suffered? And perhaps the most important question: Have my sufferings moved me to a greater love for others?

A few years ago there was a film called *How to Make an American Quilt*. Three images from the film stay with me because they reflect how we keep hope alive when time slows down because of what we are suffering.

The first image is at the very beginning of the film when we see a little girl sitting under a quilt. "For as long as I can remember," the voice of this little girl, now a grown woman, says, "my grandmother and her friends have been part of a quilting bee. I remember sitting under the quilting frame, pretending I was surrounded by a forest of friendly trees and that their stitches were messages from giants written across the sky."

When we experience suffering in our lives, we need to gather with others and remember the giants — some call them saints — in our family and faith tradition, those who teach us how to hope when there is no reason to hope. Like strong and sacred strands of thread woven into the tapestry of our personal and communal history are the names of our grandparents, mothers and fathers, aunts and uncles, sisters and brothers, teachers and listeners, community members and mentors who have died and now reside on the other side. But their names are stitched in our memory because their lives were expressions of hope for the future and courage for the present. We gather to tell their stories and draw comfort from their witness.

The second image from the film depicts Ana, the leader of the quilting bee, saying to her friends that the first thing you have to do in making a quilt is to find a theme. The theme Ana chose for her quilt was "Where Love Resides." The rest of the film tells the story of where love resides in the hearts and minds and experiences of each of those women who gather each day at the quilting frame.

"Where Love Resides" is a fitting theme to weave our lives around when suffering stops us in our tracks and derails our sense of time. We touch this residence of love within us when we acknowledge and affirm that we are God's beloved children. "See what love God has bestowed on us in letting us be called children of God!" John proclaims. "Yet that in fact is what we are" (1 John 3: 1). We have already underscored how embracing this identity is the way we find inspiration for embarking on the odyssey of grace. In fact and in faith, this is "what we are" and "who we are": God's beloved children. At no time is this realization more important than when we feel isolated and alienated by pain and suffering.

"We are God's children now," John writes. But then he adds, "what we shall later be has not yet come to light" (3: 2). This is our challenge and our hope: While we live in the darkness of our present suffering, as we embrace the hardships and struggles we endure, we will reach a moment in time — a moment of truth — when all we have experienced will come to light. As Ana tells her quilting bee friends, "The challenge with a quilt like this is that each of these squares is made by different hands, so that I have to bring all these different squares together in a balanced and harmonious design." This is the work of God's love: A greater hand than ours is at work in bringing together all our hopes and dreams, frustrations and fears into a "balanced and harmonious design."

The third image from the film occurs near the end when Ana says that in making a quilt "you have to choose your combinations carefully. The right choices will enhance your quilt, the wrong choices will dull the colors and hide their original beauty. There are no rules you can follow; you have to go by instinct, and you have to be brave."

When time stands still, when sorrow rips at our soul, stripping us of all hope, the "rules for the road" on this odyssey of grace go out the window. At these moments of time — these moments of truth — we are faced with difficult choices. We have to rely on our own instincts and on the inspiration of the Spirit. To do this we must trust our identity as God's beloved and trust that the grace of God is at work in us. This takes courage. We must be brave.

The pain and losses we experience on this odyssey of grace present us with choices. "The right choices will enhance your quilt, the wrong choices will dull the colors, hide their original beauty." Here is a story about the different choices that two women made when time stood still. One chose to try to mend the torn fabric; the other chose to spend the rest of her life as a remnant of her former self.

The Seamstress

Sarah was a seamstress. From sewing on buttons to stitching stories into the souls of those trusted friends who formed her sewing circle,

Sarah was a woman who clothed herself "with heartfelt mercy and compassion." She sewed and spun stories; she listened and mended torn fabric.

Though some might suggest that the sewing circle was nothing more than a "gab and grab the latest gossip" session, Sarah always wanted it to be more. And she wanted more people to take part in the sewing circle. She wanted it to get larger, not smaller. But since most of the women in the group were getting older, it was hard for the circle to grow. Sarah would advertise in the church bulletin but never received so much as a call from someone wanting to find out more.

Sarah helped to mend the torn fabric in family relationships by listening as she sewed. With needle and thread, open mind and open heart, Sarah made peace. Out of fragments and remnants, she stitched together reconciliation.

When Sarah died one warm summer's night, God clothed her with the seamless garment of grace because she had spent her life fashioning love in all her relationships.

At her funeral, the priest used the well-worn phrase, "A stitch in time saves nine," and played with the image of how Sarah stitched together community, was always well-prepared and looking ahead, and how now she had joined the most inclusive sewing circle of all: the communion of saints. He quoted Sarah as saying once, "Life is like a large piece of colorful cloth. I have the pattern. All I need to do is follow the pattern to make a beautiful dress."

And so it was for Sarah — through the joy and suffering and pain of her life, she followed the pattern. Life was simple and sacred.

At Sarah's funeral there was a woman named Sally. Life was not so simple and sacred for Sally. That name sounds like it should belong to someone who is bubbly and bright, always cheerful and rarely sad — someone who could take life in stride and ride out the storms with more than a measure of pleasure or patience. But Sally was anything but cheerful or patient or bubbly or bright.

When the priest looked at her at one point during his homily, he thought to himself, "If looks could kill, then this whole church would become a cemetery. Now that would be 'mass murder.' Or, if you prefer, 'murder at Mass.'" The pastor knew Sally and made a mental note to himself to ask her about the scowl on her face at Sarah's funeral.

Her eyes looked as if she was searching for a target, but the priest was grateful that the funeral mass passed without incident — or carnage.

A few days later, he ran into Sally in the supermarket and mentioned he had seen her at Sarah's funeral. "Forgive me for asking," the priest said, "but did you not feel well at the funeral? I couldn't help but notice the look on your face throughout the Mass. Is there anything wrong?"

"You made her into a saint," Sally said. "Sarah was no saint."

"Maybe not," the priest replied. "But she was certainly closer than most."

But Sally was unmoved. "You don't know the whole story," she said abruptly and pushed her cart down the aisle toward the frozen food.

The next Wednesday afternoon, the priest made it a point to stop by the sewing circle to see if he could find out why Sally was so upset with Sarah. Since it was the first meeting of the sewing circle since Sarah's death, there were many stories shared around the circle. When the stories seemed to be winding down, the priest asked innocently, "I saw Sally at Sarah's funeral, and she looked very upset."

As soon as Sally's name was mentioned, the needles and threads seemed to stop in unison. The ladies looked at one another. What should they do? Should they say anything? Would they be breaking the seal of the sewing circle if they told the priest what happened between Sarah and Sally?

Finally, clearing her throat, Sarah's best friend, Clara, said, "Father, you have to understand that both Sarah and Sally lost their husbands around the same time. This was long before you came to the parish. Lord have mercy, it must have been twenty-five years ago."

"Twenty-six," a voice from across the room belonging to Mildred corrected Clara. "Sarah's husband died on a Monday, and Sally's husband ran off with Flo, the waitress at the diner, on a Friday. She never got over it."

Well, the priest began to hear more about the waitress named Flo and Sally's ex-husband than he ever wanted to know. So pretending that he had to leave, he interrupted the sewing circle's true confessions and said, "But why did Sally resent Sarah so much?"

"Oh, Father," Clara said. "Isn't it obvious? Sarah handled her loss so much better than Sally did. Now, granted, their losses were different. Sarah's husband died of a heart attack, and Sally's husband left her. But while Sarah started this sewing circle as a way to handle her grief, Sally didn't know what to do. She just became more bitter with every passing day."

"Sarah surely tried to help Sally," Mildred chimed in. "She invited her to join the sewing circle, and Sally came quite regularly at the beginning. But she was always so negative. She was just filled with bitterness. And one day, Sarah politely said something to her about being so negative all the time. And that was it. We never saw Sally at the sewing circle again."

Another woman in the group added that Sally never spoke to them for several years. "I was surprised she came to the funeral," Clara said. "She's just so bitter."

The priest thanked the women for telling him the story. "I guess it's not true what they say about time healing all wounds," he said.

Sally was the remnant, the torn piece of fabric, that Sarah wanted so much to mend. "Sarah always felt the sewing circle wasn't complete until Sally came back," Clara said. "She died before she could complete the circle."

Suffering levels the landscape. Except that no suffering is the same. It is how we handle the pain and loss of our lives that makes all the difference. That sewing circle provided a safe place where the wounds of life could be transformed into garments of grace. In this safe place, secrets could be shared — fears and tears, too. But while Sarah and the other women found in each other soul mates through the stories they told and the wine of compassion they shared, Sally only tasted the sour grapes of her own betrayal and loss.

Navel Gazing and Star Gazing

In every situation of suffering we are given a choice. We can spend our time navel gazing, or we can spend our time star gazing. In most instances, both are worthwhile activities that reflect saving graces.

When a child is born and the cord is cut, one's connection to one's mother — to the source of life — is always marked upon one's body. This becomes a symbol of how we are connected to the source of our lives. We have the marks on our bodies to prove it.

Sometimes we can be dismissed by others as always "navel gazing." It is a legitimate charge if all we do is look inside and never go out to meet others in their need. But when we suffer a loss, we need to spend at least some time navel gazing to see what's going on inside. In one sense, didn't Jesus do some navel gazing in the garden as he looked into the cup of suffering and said, "If it is possible, let this cup pass me by. But let it be as you would have it, not I" (Luke 22: 42)? He was about to be arrested for speaking the truth. He was about to die for crimes of compassion. Looking at the face of death reflected in the cup of suffering, isn't it possible Jesus asked himself, "Was this what I came to do? Is this how it's supposed to end? Am I doing this out of love? Will this really bring about a new creation? Will my death bring others life?"

Christians believe that Jesus writes his answers to those questions with his blood on a cross. What did he come to do? Jesus came to save the world. What did he come to learn? He came to learn what it means to be human. He came to love all people made in the image and likeness of God and awaken the awareness of our true identity as God's beloved children. Jesus came to heal the earth.

These questions become more focused for those who stand at the crossroads of a terminal illness. In one sense, Jesus was facing a terminal illness when his tears became like drops of blood in the garden. He knew his life on earth was about to end. Those who face a terminal situation face these questions squarely. What is the point of my life? Why was I born? What difference did I make? Are others better because I was part of their lives, because they were touched by mine? How am I changed? What have I learned? Whom have I loved? Whom do I love?

When one is running out of time, these questions keep time on one's mind. Maybe this is a good time to ask, "Who are the people who form my sewing circle?" Both living and deceased, who are the people who form the circle of my life and keep me safe?

All of us face these questions in one form or fashion each day of our lives, but they become very focused when we are challenged by time limits. We only have so much time. This is why it is so important to navel gaze now and then — to zero in on our core realities — especially when we are experiencing the limits of time.

Yet we must also see the bigger picture of how our little lives fit into God's plan of salvation. When we only navel gaze, we can miss the grand scheme of salvation that God has written not only on our bodies but also in the stars. Remember God taking Abraham outside and telling him to look at the stars. The covenant of love is written across the sky.

I am told that if you stand in the bottom of a well, you will be able to see the stars even in the daytime. I have not tested this theory. Though I've spent some time now and then at the bottom of a well, I've normally been sitting. I'm not sure you can stand at the bottom of a well unless you're lowered very carefully from above. Most of the time those who find themselves at the bottom of a well are deposited there by other folks. They are tossed into the bottom of the well to get them out of the way or because they are the object of envy or suspicion or fear. Joseph's brothers threw him there because they were envious of his dreams and his "favorite son" status with their father.

If one is thrown into a well, one would likely land on one's head. Can we see the stars while standing on our head? My limited experience of standing at the bottom of a well is that we're more likely to see scars than stars. Scars are illuminated in the darkness. Suffering is like infrared light that highlights our scars. They say, though, that when someone's been knocked out, say, in a heavyweight fight, the person sees stars.

Standing at the bottom of a well seems to afford a similar experience.

But whether we see stars or scars, both are signs of God's covenant. The stars reflect the first covenant God made with our ancestors in faith when he told Abraham and Sarah that their descendants would be as numerous as the stars (see Genesis 15: 5). The scars reflect the new covenant God made with us when after his resurrection Jesus shows his disciples his wounds, breathes on them and says, "Receive the Holy Spirit" (John 20: 22).

Whether we stand in a well and look up to see the stars or look into our own souls and see scars, we see signs of God's covenant and, in these moments of truth, also discover we have landed in the lap of grace.

Where Does It Hurt?

This leap of grace into the lap of God brings to mind a question our mothers asked us when we were sick to our stomach or feeling out of sorts for one reason or another: "Where does it hurt?" When we are older, the question may come from a doctor, nurse or a friend — someone who is willing to touch the wound or examine it for swelling or a bruise.

When we have been hurt in a relationship or betrayed by a friend, it may be too early to see a scar. And sometimes the wounds inflicted by life don't leave a scar. At least on the skin.

Only on the soul.

Every wound leaves a scar somewhere.

We anoint the place where it hurts and hope like heaven that healing happens. But when it does not, we can live with it because we anointed the place where it hurts. Anointing brings healing in one way or another. This is what grace does. In the words of Mari West Zimmerman, grace "proclaims our innocence and anoints our loss. What we've endured to reach this place, this Holy of Holies where time ends and God's kingdom begins," enables us to rise "into the mystery of present salvation."

The little aches and pains, bumps and bruises we experience along the way reflect how we live such small lives, filled with our tiny terrors and little victories and hollow defeats. Yet we are not saved "little by little," but once and for all. If we truly believed we are saved by a force of love larger than ourselves, then we could live day by day anointing each loss with love, crowning each gain with laughter, and doing what our mothers used to tell us to do when we were sick: "offer it up."

And move on.

But what about those larger losses that leave a deep and gaping hole in the pit of our soul? Do we simply "offer them up" too? Those who suffer chronic illnesses sometimes say — not in a pious way but with a firm conviction of faith — that they hope their suffering will help someone who needs it. Many spiritual writers have posited the promise that when we unite our suffering and sorrows with others in the world who are in pain, the force of grace moves us toward the fulfillment of God's reign. In *Hymn of the Universe*, Teilhard de Chardin writes:

> Suffering holds hidden within it...the ascensional force of the world. The whole point is to set this force free by making it conscious of what it signifies and of what it is capable. For if all the sick people in the world were simultaneously to turn their sufferings into a single shared longing for the speedy completion of the kingdom of God...what a vast leap towards God the world would make.

For this leap of grace to occur, we must be willing to unite our sufferings into one cup and lift it up to our God. In doing so, our prayer becomes the same prayer Jesus voiced in the garden: "Thy kindom come, thy will be done."

So, where does it hurt?

Time may take the sting out of an old wound, but contrary to popular prescriptions about time's healing qualities, the passage of time will not always heal a wound. After a while, the place where the wound was inflicted will become more like a dull ache than a sharp stab, but the scar will survive. Yet one day healing can happen. Healing can take place in time.

When that healing time does come, we realize, in the words of Rumi, "Where there is ruin, there is hope for a treasure."

The Force of Grace: The Last Supper

We see how Jesus placed all the hopes and hurts of a broken world and of his own broken heart in one cup and lifted it up on the night he was betrayed. Then he invited his disciples to place their lives in the cup and drink from it. The strength of this symbol of placing our lives in one cup, offering it up to God in prayer and then drinking from it was brought home to me a few years ago when Father Gene LaVerdiere, a noted Scripture scholar, spoke at a meeting of my religious community. During that meeting we were addressing some of the issues that were causing divisions in our community. We invited Father LaVerdiere to help us make some connections between what we were experiencing as a community of faith and the spirituality of the blood of Christ inherent in our name *The Precious Blood Communiy*.

One of the more helpful insights he gave us, however, was not a connection but a distinction. He made a distinction between the "Lord's Supper" and the "Last Supper." He pointed out there "there are many ways we can assemble, but to assemble as church means being open to all." He challenged us to remember that when we assemble as church, the boundaries are extended, the barricades come down and the barriers disappear. All must feel welcome. "It's easy to assemble as a cozy group," Father LaVerdiere said, "but very difficult to assemble as church."

The Scripture reference point for this distinction is Paul's first letter to the Corinthians. There was much dissension within the faith community at Corinth. Paul says plainly, "There are divisions among you" (1 Corinthians 1: 11). The source of these divisions, LaVerdiere explained, was the "house churches" that had formed in allegiance to either Apollos, Cephas or Paul. When the members of these house churches gathered together in assembly, divisions and factions began to appear. Paul's criticism of these assemblies was direct: "Is Christ divided? Was Paul crucified for you? Or were you baptized in the name of Paul?" (1: 13).

I knew there were differences existing among the members of my religious community, but when we gathered for that assembly I was surprised and saddened by how deep those divisions seemed to be. On the first evening of the assembly, we gathered in small groups and were invited to write down words to describe our positive and negative views about where we presently were as a community. We then took these words written on yellow and green cards and hung them on red ribbons suspended from the ceiling. They looked like dangling threads from a frayed tapestry. As I recall, the negatives were written on yellow cards and the positives on green cards.

Then, after we had hung up our yellow and green cards, we were given a chance to speak our minds and maybe what was in our hearts. All who spoke were certainly courageous in doing so. But when the first six or seven speakers at the issues forum chose to reflect the messages written on the yellow cards, I wondered if we were making reservations at the Lord's Supper or our own supper. I wondered if we were simply rehearsing our personal, exclusive concerns.

After naming these issues, we didn't process what was being raised but simply ritualized our concerns by placing them in the cup. After the ritual, I tasted more yellow than green. The aftertaste was bitter. I suffered from indigestion for the rest of the assembly, carrying a burning in the pit of my stomach and a heaviness in my heart.

The Mystery of Suffering: Go Deeper

This was not the first time we had been over all these issues that divide us. Perhaps my indigestion came from the fact that we had made so little progress from the assembly a few years before this one where we spent four days addressing our wounds. At the time, the intent of the provincial council was not to heal the wounds but to provide a safe place where the wounds could be opened, reverenced and treated with the balm we call charity.

The experience reminded me that there is a difference between naming the wounds and seeing them as a means of transformation. We can name the problems and the pains in our lives and our world until we are sick to our stomach and sick to our soul. But the sickness will persist unless we allow them to be a means to help us grow in grace.

It's like the old story about the difference between a thermometer and a thermostat. Both read the temperature. Both can tell you whether a room is hot or cold. But all the thermometer does is tell the temperature. The thermostat not only reads the temperature; it also sets in motion the forces that will bring the room to an acceptable climate. We have more than enough thermometers in our world, in our churches, communities, workplaces and families. We have more than enough people who can tell us what's wrong with the world. What we need are more thermostats who will set in motion the forces of love that will bring our places of worship and work to a climate where the truth about our wounds can be told and healing can occur.

A friend once told me that her dentist had performed a root canal on her, but because the dentist didn't want to hurt her, she didn't go deep enough. This caused an abscess that made a second root canal necessary. This friend concluded: "Pain is essential to get it all out."

Are we willing to go deeper into the pain and excise the abscess? That seems to be the question that surfaced for me in the weeks following the assembly where Father LaVerdiere invited us to drink from the cup at the Lord's Supper and not our own supper. We were still drinking from the cups that clutter the tables of our own little worlds — separate tables and separate cups.

The cup from which Jesus invites us to drink at every Eucharist is the cup of suffering and blessing. But we'll never taste the blessing unless we go deeper into the issue of belonging. This was — and, to some degree, still is — the issue facing my own religious community. But perhaps it is also a question that faces all the "sewing circles" to which we belong. Do we really have a sense of belonging — a "longing to be" with one another? Do we want to be and breathe together? When we are together, are we really present to one another? Do we want to be present to one another?

In the lyrics of the theme song from the old television show *Cheers*, do we have a place "where everybody knows our name"? And in this place, can we tell our truth because we trust those to whom we belong and thus know it is a safe place?

If we want to confront the factions and divisions that exist among us, we must delve ever deeper into the mystery of our identity and our relationship with those with whom we walk on this odyssey of grace. The reality of reconciliation within a community depends on our willingness to name and claim the truth. In this moment of truth we ask: Is there a group to which we belong, a community, a "sewing circle," that is a safe enough place for the truth to be spoken? These issues of belonging, of identity, of the mystery and meaning of relationship, cut deeply into our collective soul, causing our souls to bleed. But if we are going to live on the cutting edge of the faith community and the culture, then we can expect a little blood now and then.

Or are we afraid of the sight of blood?

This is where our odyssey of grace will ultimately lead us — to the very edge of time and space. If we are not willing to go where the spirit of God wills us to go, then we should be honest and name the fear. If we are not ready to live on the edge, we should step back and move to that place where we define "feeling safe" by staying on the surface. It's okay to stay a while longer in this "safe" place where all the wounds have bandages and no one faints at the sight of blood because there is no blood in sight. Just remember what Rumi wrote about that "bandaged place": "That's where the light enters you." It's where the light enters if we can keep our wounds open.

It is in that wounded place where saving grace begins to filter in as light. But it takes time and it takes patience and a willingness to take enormous risks to cultivate the kind of relationships that afford one the safety to acknowledge a deep wound. If this wound is reverenced without others trying to heal it too quickly, we have found a sewing circle that will over time help us to take even more risks. But if others dismiss the wound by saying it's no big deal or "get over it and get on with your life," it is likely that the bandage will go back in place and the wound will only deepen.

When this happens, it doesn't necessarily mean we'll never find our common ground on the cutting edge of truth. Remember, to find common ground each of us has to give a little ground, die a little bit. As Father LaVerdiere reminded us, "There's a lot of dying to do to drink the cup." Maybe I need to die to my particular vision of how we can find our home, find each other, on the edge. I know I need to die to the attitude of arrogance in me that tempts me to believe I can be comfortable living on the edge. There's nothing comfortable about living on the fringe. It's sharp. It's dangerous. Its jagged edges cut and cause us to bleed.

But that's the point at which we pass the cup to catch the blood. "This cup which is poured out for you is the new covenant in my blood" (Luke 22: 20). When we gather at Eucharist to drink from the cup, these are the words that move our memories and stir our imaginations. They remind us that when we gather it is not our supper but the Lord's Supper. If it is only our supper, then it's much easier to be exclusive, to hold on to our differences, to stay on the surface and to leave the table whenever we feel like it.

But if it's the Lord's Supper, then we do what he did. He stayed at the table in the company of friends even though one of these friends would betray him, another would deny him, and the rest would argue among themselves about who was making the most important contribution to the community. Remember how in Luke's account, immediately after inviting his disciples to drink from the cup "in remembrance of me," he announces: "Behold, the hand of him who betrays me is with me on the table" (Luke 22: 21). Then, after each disciple denies he is the culprit, "a dispute also arose among them" about "which of them was to be regarded as the greatest" (22: 24).

On this odyssey of grace, we are called to walk and to live on the edge. When we stop along the way and sit at the table of community to break bread and pass around the cup of wine, we do so in memory of the one who called us to make this journey. It is the Lord's Supper and not our own. We are to drink deeply of the pain and the promise, the loneliness and the laughter, the lethargy and the energy of each one who places his or her life in the cup. And we taste our own pain and promise too. Then we boldly offer it to God with the hope that through the grace and mercy of God, the kindom not only will come but has come. It comes when we pass this cup around at the table in the company of friends at the Lord's Supper.

Psalm: Sacred Threads in Time

Grandmother God,
Queen Bee of the Quilting Circle,
we recall with gratitude
all those holy women and men
who have touched our lives with their grace and love.
By remembering their sacred stories,
their lives are woven into the fabric of our faith.
Threads of meaning and memory
are stitched into this quilt of our family and community.

We give you thanks, O Queen of all days and nights,
for your Son, the Sewer,
whose stitch in time saved more than nine lives,
and for all those sacred seamstresses,
the crowd of witnesses whose lives
reflect what it means to be poor in spirit,
merciful and just,
humble and holy servants of Christ
and children of God.

Gracious Grandma God,
we wrap ourselves with this quilt of many colors
that gives us comfort on the coldest nights.
With you as our Divine Comforter,
we shall live in the warm embrace
of your benevolent grace.

Chapter Eight

Time on Our Hands:
Grace in Action

God called the world into being and that call continues.
There is this present moment because God is present.
Every instant is an act of creation...
Time is God's gift to the world of space...
This is the task of humans:
To conquer space and sanctify time...
—Abraham Heschel

If you look deeply into the palm of your hand,
you will see your parents and all generations of your ancestors.
—Thich Nhat Hanh

See, upon the palms of my hands I have written your name.
—Isaiah 49: 16

As we travel through the various states of grace in our lives, we will notice that we have time on our hands. Don't wash it off! Instead of washing our hands when we have the chance, it's really time to wash a few feet. This is how we sanctify time: serving one another with love.

Grace and time go together — hand in hand. But until we learn a sense of timing, the question "What time is it?" will cause us to look immediately at our wrist where our watch is.

But Time will tell us, "Don't look at your watch. Look at your hands."

Time is on our hands. We look for it but can't see it. We protest, "But we don't have any time on our hands. Can't you see it's gone? Time has disappeared. We are too busy. We have washed our hands with our work. There's not enough time. There's never enough time."

But rather than viewing the hands of time as the enemy ready to grab us by the throat or stop us in our tracks or push us over the edge, we might view the hands of time as a friend who will catch us when we fall.

When Father Leo Brand, a priest in my community, was told he had three to six months to live, he said to me, "God has given me the gift of time to get my house in order." He was given less than six months of life, and he looked at it as a "gift" of time. He did not look at his diagnosis as a death sentence but as a life sentence. He looked at the time he had remaining as graced. At the end of his life, Leo did something most of us rarely do — he measured time by the minute and treasured every moment.

This is the work of our hands: not to wring our hands with regret or frustration but to wrap our hands about God's grace and hang on for the ride of our lives. This is the work of our hands: not to close our hands in a fist that resists reconciliation but to open our hands in a sign of peace.

Grace: A Hands-on Activity

A few years ago, there was a film called *Patch Adams*. An image in the film reflects well what we do when we have time on our hands. In an early scene Patch has committed himself to a mental institution because of depression. There he encounters an eccentric old man in a wheelchair who is always holding up four fingers and asking anyone who will listen, "How many fingers do you see?" The obvious answer is "Four." But when the man hears that response, he huffs and puffs and wheels himself away in frustration.

One night Patch is in this old man's room, and once again the old man holds up four fingers. Patch can't see what the old man is getting at so his answer is the same as he's always given: "You're holding up four fingers." The old man tells him to look again. Don't focus on the problem, the old man says, but the person. Don't look at the fingers, look at me. Sure enough, Patch looks beyond the four fingers to the old man. With his eyes focused on the person rather than the problem, he sees what the old man has been getting at. In the old man's eyes he sees eight fingers, not four! This was the breakthrough Patch needed to begin to see life in a new way. He began to focus his energies not on problems but on people.

This is the invitation of grace: to see with new eyes, to think in new ways and to become a new creation. Grace invites us to see not problems but people, not just symptoms of a disease but the sacred dignity of each human being, not just illnesses but the image of God that beats within every heart. With the help of God's grace, we begin to see with new eyes that allow us to embrace the diversity among us and see it as a gift rather than as a threat to our unity. Grace dares us to take a longer view and have a larger vision of ourselves and our world.

On this grace odyssey, we are invited to take a hands-on approach to the problems and pain we experience in our own lives and in the lives of those we encounter along the way. Grace is a hands-on activity. So, if we have the time, there is a lot of work to do — the work of grace.

I propose we do this work by taking that image of the old man holding up four fingers and apply it to a four-finger approach to grace. In addition to these four fingers, there is also the basic "rule of thumb" that will offer others a sign of peace. This is a "hands-on" approach to the ministry of grace.

Throughout the Gospels, Jesus' healing ministry is a "hands-on" activity. A Gospel story that comes to mind is the one in which Jesus encounters a man with a withered hand. The story goes that on the Sabbath when Jesus is praying and teaching in the Temple, a man with a withered hand comes to him for healing. Those who oppose Jesus wonder if he will cure the man with the withered hand since it is unlawful to do so on the Sabbath. Jesus notices his adversaries' intense interest in this case. They seem to be waiting to charge Jesus with spiritual malpractice. Jesus knows what they are up to, so he asks them, "Is it lawful to do good or to do harm on the Sabbath, to save life or to kill?" (Mark 3: 4).

Jesus' question to the Pharisees leaves them speechless. Their silence and their lack of compassion anger him and grieve him. The man standing next to Jesus has a withered hand, but the Pharisees are suffering from an even more serious affliction: a withered heart. They're afflicted with hardening of the arteries leading to their hearts. Their hearts are hard. Their arteries were clogged with so much suspicion and legality, fear and hypocrisy, that even the divine healer isn't able to break up the blocked paths to their hearts.

So Jesus focuses instead on what he can do. He says to the man with the withered hand, "Stretch out your hand" (3: 5). This man who has walked through life with a clenched fist can feel the blood flowing to his fingers as he opens his hand.

On the other hand, the Pharisees have walked through life with a clenched heart. In telling the man to stretch out his hand, we can almost hear Jesus saying to the Pharisees, "Stretch out your hearts." As they watch Jesus cure the man with the withered hand — a healing that is spiritual as well as physical as Jesus returns the man to wholeness — the Pharisees sit on their hands. They will not raise their hands to show support, or lend a hand to help Jesus heal, or even clap their hands in a sign of affirmation and appreciation for the miraculous healing. Because their hearts remain hard, they keep their hands to themselves — which, of course, is the opposite of compassion. When we keep our hands to ourselves because of the hardness of our own hearts, our bodies speak the language of indifference to someone for whom our compassion could make a difference.

What do we see when we look at our hands? As the man whose hand was withered looked upon his fingers and palm, now restored to wholeness, perhaps for the first time he could see his soul. Look closely. It was widely believed in ancient times that when one made something with one's hands, one infused the creation with a piece of one's soul.

We are made in God's image, permeated with God's presence. The divine imprint is upon our bodies and our souls. We bear the marks of the Divine One — God's fingerprints are all over us. In the same way, in everything we create, we leave our fingerprints and a piece of our soul. As no two people share the same fingerprints, so each of us is unique. Whatever — and whomever — we touch in our lives, we leave behind a part of our very selves.

Or perhaps when the man with the withered hand stretched out his hand, he saw the common ground signified by his palm. An open hand can give another a sign of peace, a handshake of welcome, a greeting of affirmation. But when that palm is concealed, as it had been for him, shriveled and withered for years, when the fingers are closed over that palm and made into a fist, it means there is no common ground.

From one perspective, what all this suggests is that when we look at our hands, we see the sacred connection with our ancestors, with our own spiritual histories that have fashioned our faith. We look at our hands and see how everything and everyone we touch flows from the depth of our souls and is released through our fingertips. We look at our hands and remember how each of us and all of us are held in the hands of a compassionate God, our names inscribed in the palm of God's hand.

This is the place where the work of grace and the work of our hands come together. Now let's look closely at this four-finger and rule of thumb approach to the ministry of grace.

A Handful of Grace
String Finger: Remembering the Story

The first finger in this hands-on approach to the ministry of grace points to the past. Like people who tie a string to their finger to remind them of something they have to do or someone they have to see, in the ministry of grace we call to mind the story of how God has acted in our past. We might call this our "string" finger because it reminds us how memory plays an important role in the work of grace.

In Luke's Gospel, for example, memory plays an important part in the core Christian story of resurrection. "They remembered Jesus' words" (24: 8), Luke writes of the women who visited the tomb at dawn on the first day of the week. Luke's version of the Easter events focuses on Joanna, Mary Magdalene and the other women who followed Jesus to the end. These are the same women Jesus stopped to console as he made his way to Calvary. These are the same women who stood at a distance to watch and to pray during the horror of that Friday afternoon. These are the same women who did not run away but stayed. These same women went to the garden early Sunday morning and "found the stone rolled away from the tomb; but when they entered, they did not find the body of Jesus" (24: 2-3).

Luke reports that the women were puzzled. What must have gone through their minds? Did they come to the wrong tomb? Did someone steal the body? How could anyone lose or misplace a body? As these questions whirled around inside their heads, their hearts received an angelic answer: "Why do you seek the living one among the dead? He is not here, but he has been raised up. Remember what he said to you while he was still in Galilee, that the Chosen One must be handed over...be crucified...and rise on the third day" (24: 5-7).

When Joanna, Mary Magdalene and the other women heard these words, their hearts were stirred with memory. "And they remembered his words."

Resurrection has a lot to do with remembering. Because these women who heard the words of the angels at the tomb remembered Jesus' words, they ran off to tell the others. Unfortunately, unlike the women, the men had not tied a string to their finger. Rather, in their grief and guilt, their disappointment and even despair, they were not only suffering from a memory lapse but a memory loss.

In Luke's telling of the story, the women told the disciples huddled in hopelessness in the upper room the story of all they had seen and heard at the tomb. "But these words seemed to them an idle tale, and they did not believe them" (24: 11). The men thought the story was an "idle tale," and you know what they say about "idle hands" being the devil's playground. The men kept their idle hands to themselves and so stopped the flow of grace. But the women had tied a string to their finger and remembered the story.

Indeed, the reason the women's story seemed so far-fetched to the very practical and factual disciples is because of memory failure. The disciples thought the story sounded like nonsense. But they forgot that so much of the Jesus story didn't make reasonable sense. For example, remember the story of the son demanding his share of his father's inheritance — in effect telling his dad, "I wish you were dead." Then, after running off and wasting all the money he "comes to his senses."

When he returns home with a contrite heart and a well-rehearsed act of contrition, the father runs out to meet him and welcomes him home. It doesn't make any sense that the father should spend more on this spoiled brat. It doesn't make sense that he should be on the lookout for this wayward one and then run out to meet him instead of waiting for him to grovel and beg forgiveness. It doesn't make any sense!

Or remember the story about the woman who loses a precious coin turning her house upside down in order to find this lost coin. What nonsense — just leave it be and it will turn up.

Does it make any sense that a shepherd would leave the ninety-nine sheep unprotected while going off in search of the one that got away? Where is this shepherd's common sense?

Remember this about grace: It doesn't make any sense! It is a free gift from a gracious God. The disciples forgot that none of this odyssey of faith makes any sense unless we remember the whole story, unless we remember his words.

Thank God that Mary Magdalene, Joanna and the other women had a good memory. Because they remembered the words of Jesus, what seemed like nonsense to the men made perfect sense to them.

For Christians, the journey of faith makes no sense without the resurrection. And resurrection seems like nonsense without faith. Indeed, resurrection will make little sense even to people of faith if they fail to remember the whole story. The primary reason for keeping this memory alive is so we can tell the story again and again when we need to hear it, when we're suffering from lapses of memory or even memory loss. In those times when we are lost in the dark or losing hope because of the chaos in our lives, we tell the story of how God created holy order out of utter chaos with those first words attributed to God in the Scriptures: "Let there be light" (Genesis 1: 14).

When we feel imprisoned by fear or enslaved by our work or chained to our desk or oppressed by our church, we remember the story of how a ragtag group of slaves escaped a powerful army. It doesn't make any sense that a defenseless people should escape a mighty machinery of war described in the book of Exodus with the military mantra "chariots and charioteers" (Exodus 14: 9-28). It doesn't make any sense that the wind should be so strong and create a wall of water at just the right time so that this motley band of nomads could cross on dry land. It seems like nonsense that the wind would die down just when they had reached a safe place so that the wall of water would fall on the mighty military in hot pursuit.

Does it make any sense that God should choose a barren couple old enough to have great grandchildren to be parents for the first time? And not just parents of a few children but of "countless generations" (Genesis 3: 16). Does it make any sense that a fugitive should become a fearless prophet as a result of something that makes no sense at all: a burning bush not consumed by fire? Does it make any sense that a humble young maiden should be visited by an angel and say yes to a plan only God could conceive?

We remember and tell these stories of faith because we know that none of this makes any sense without the grace of God. These are simply idle tales that make no sense if we do not tie a string to our finger and remember how this odyssey of faith is rooted in our common memory — the stories of God's uncommon commitment to the people of the earth from the beginning of creation. In these remembered stories we discover our common sense. And didn't our moms and dads always tell us to use our common sense? Our common sense says that God continues to be faithful to us no matter how often we fail.

There are so many things in life that don't make sense. When confronted with tragedies like the sudden death of someone we love, tragedies that transcend our grasp and may cause us to lose our sense of reality, it's wise to tie a string to our finger. And remember the story. Or, like Peter, we can go to the place from which the women came, peer inside, and see if the sights and sounds and smells might jog our memory. Then, like Peter, we will "go home amazed at what happened" (Luke 24: 12).

That's because what we celebrate on this odyssey of faith is God's amazing grace. It's only through the grace of God that any of this makes any sense. We cooperate with God's amazing grace when we remember the stories and find our place in them.

Then it all begins to make sense again.

Trigger Finger: Touching the Wound

With our second finger, we touch the wounds and the wonders in our own experiences. We usually use the word "touch" to describe the experience of empathy. We say a story or a song or a film "touched" us, and we mean that we experienced a movement of the soul and of the heart. We may say we were "moved" when another came to share our burden or gave us a word of encouragement.

On the other hand, when something touches us in a painful way, when our skin is burned or wounded or bleeding from a scrape or a cut or a bruise, we feel it far beneath the surface of our skin. Such a painful touch reaches to the core of who we are, shakes us, startles us, and reminds us how truly fragile we are. That is why this particular finger of our hands-on approach to grace reflects in a very precise way who we are: "fragile — handle with care."

The touch of a hand is a powerful means of expressing compassion. With this finger, we point to a broken heart. With our finger we trace the breaks in our own experience, because it is through the cracks of our broken heart that God's grace can get inside.

Compassion begins with our own experience of a broken heart. But when our hearts are broken, we are faced with a choice. We can either keep the broken space open, or we can shut down completely. As we saw in the story of the man with the withered hand, an open hand, an open palm, symbolizes an open heart. When our hearts are open, our hands will be too. But if our hearts are closed, we will walk through life with clenched fists. My experience has been that people who truly listen with sensitivity are people who allow their own experiences of sorrow and suffering to keep their hearts open. They are actively engaged in listening to the pain of others because of their own experiences of sorrow.

The danger, of course, is that when we actively listen with sensitivity and compassion, we can allow so much of others' suffering into the broken spaces of our own hearts that there is no more room. We have to shut down or else our hearts will become so heavy with the weight of sorrow that we can no longer open our hands and hearts to anyone.

When we listen with a compassionate heart, we have to let go of the need for answers. We have to let go of the urgency to make sense out of the situation and to fix the other's problem or heal the breach in the other's heart. When we actively listen to another with sensitivity and sincerity, we suspend the necessity to know the answers and simply meet the other person in this place of pain. This compassionate presence will be more than enough because the other isn't looking for a cure so much as he or she is looking for a companion.

This is the place where Jesus meets the disciples after his resurrection. In Luke's version of this story (24: 36-49), after Jesus appears to the disciples on the road to Emmaus, he appears to his fearful friends in the upper room. Remember that they didn't believe the women's story about the empty tomb because it sounded like "an idle tale." They are still suffering from amnesia when Jesus appears to them but "in their panic and fright they thought they were seeing a ghost" (24: 37). Can we imagine the look on the faces of these disciples? We probably can because we sometimes say to a person who has been startled or surprised, "You look like you've seen a ghost." But when Jesus appears in that upper room, he is very real and he wants his disciples to understand the reality of resurrection.

Jesus does two things to dispel the notion that they are seeing a ghost: He shows them his wounds and asks for something to eat. These two "ghostbusting" activities — touching the wounds and sharing a meal — are used often in the resurrection accounts. We might call them "touch and tell" techniques to convince those who are skeptical that the resurrection is real and not some kind of divine magic trick. He invites his disciples to trace the scars on his body and to tell the stories of life over a meal so they would know they were not having a holy hallucination. They needed to know that the resurrected Jesus was not just a figment of their imaginations and their grieving spirits.

In our "hands-on" approach to ministry, this second finger of grace traces the wounds, and in the scars and the stories we find meaning and a measure of hope.

But it is important to remember that when we help another trace the break in his or her broken heart, we will encounter more than sorrow and sadness; we will also encounter skepticism. How can I ever love again after my heart has been broken? How can I ever trust again after I have been betrayed? How can I live when the person I loved the most in the world has died?

Certainly the disciples were skeptical. They didn't believe the women, and now they have a hard time believing they are not seeing a ghost. As he eats a piece of cooked fish, Jesus uses the second finger of grace by saying, "Recall those words I spoke to you while I was still with you" (24: 44). We could call this the "trigger finger" of grace because Jesus points to the stories he told before he died, trying to trigger the disciples' memory.

When we hear that phrase "trigger finger," we think of a gunslinger or perhaps of wounds inflicted by someone who uses his or her trigger finger to do violence. But Jesus uses his trigger finger not only to activate the disciples' memory but also to get them to touch his wounds. He has to do this because something has obviously changed about Jesus. He's not the same, or else he wouldn't have used the phrase, "while I was still with you." His bodily appearance has obviously changed. He doesn't look the same as he did before he died.

This makes sense, doesn't it? Our physical bodies limit us. Time and space limit us. But now in his new, resurrected form, though his body bears the marks of crucifixion, he is not confined or imprisoned by the wounds. Rather, they inspire him to be available in every situation where hearts are broken and wounds are inflicted. Jesus is no longer limited by time and space but is now capable of being present whenever and wherever he is needed. And this is a real presence, as evidenced by his scars and his hunger pangs.

Our ancestors in faith did not believe in ghosts but in a real presence that transforms our bodies and souls and makes us "witnesses of all these things" (Luke 24: 48). So even if at times we look like we've seen a ghost, we continue to engage in ghostbusting techniques that give witness to the resurrection of Jesus by creating safe places where we can trace the wounds by sharing our faith stories and telling the truth. It is in these moments of truth that we find the reality that will set us free from the past. We will also experience a compassionate presence and a measure of courage to face the future.

Pointing Finger: Looking to the Future

If the first finger, the string finger, points to the past and the second finger, the trigger finger, points to the wounds where we find compassionate presence, the third finger points to the future. Though most of us were told when we were young that it's not polite to point a finger at anyone, we call this our "pointing" finger because it reflects our desire in the ministry of grace to point to the presence of God's forgiveness.

We can point out peoples' faults and point our fingers to blame and to shame. But this finger in our hands-on approach to grace points out that the future is great for those who know God's mercy and share it with others.

We discover this third finger of grace in the story of Mary Magdalene seeing Jesus that morning of his resurrection but mistaking him for the gardener (John 20: 11-18). Mary recognizes the Risen Christ when Jesus calls her by name. Then she is told not to cling to Jesus but to "go and tell others" (20: 17).

Mary Magdalene is one of those women who remembered the story. She is the focus of John's account of Jesus' first appearance after the resurrection. But when Mary encounters the Risen Jesus, she thinks he is the gardener. It is not a stretch for Mary to believe that Jesus is a gardener because John's story of Jesus' passion and death begins and ends in a garden. "Jesus went out with his disciples across the Kidron Valley to where there was a garden" (John 18: 1). John reports that Judas knew this place "because Jesus had often met there with his disciples" (18: 2). The same motivation of selfishness and sin, of pride and perhaps greed, that led to Adam and Eve's eviction notice from the garden in Genesis leads to Jesus' arrest in the garden in John's Gospel. After he is tried and tortured, convicted and executed, John notes that "in the place where he was crucified there was a garden, and in the garden a new tomb, in which no one had yet been buried" (19: 41).

Like the first creation that began with a garden, so the new creation also comes from a garden.

Indeed, this image of Jesus as a gardener is a good one since the Christian faith story begins in the Garden of Eden. It is fitting that the most important truth of the Christian faith — that through the life, death and resurrection of Jesus sin and death have been conquered forever — should occur in a garden. Maybe Mary thinking Jesus was the gardener is not really a case of mistaken identity after all. In truth, "after the fall" it takes someone like a gardener who is not afraid of getting his hands dirty in the soil of the earth to redeem the earth and all its creatures.

However, the stone-cold empty tomb has caused an April frost to descend upon Mary's heart until her heart is warmed by hearing this gardener say her name, "Mary" (20: 16). At the sound of her name, Mary recognizes Jesus.

The Risen One doesn't go so far as to sing to Mary the old nursery rhyme, "Mary, Mary, quite contrary, how does your garden grow?" because he knows. When Mary's eyes are opened and she recognizes the Risen One, Jesus says to her, "Do not cling to me. Rather go and tell the others" (20: 17). This garden grows by our going out to tell others. By planting in the hearts of others the joy of our belief in eternal life, the garden of God's goodness will grow. Sharing this good news with others will cause this garden to grow beyond our wildest expectations.

The story says that our personal encounter with the Risen One carries with it the same command: "Go and tell others." The future is in our hands. When we hear the sound of our name spoken in the whisper of the wind or the laughter of children or the tenderness of our beloved, we find the grace to go forth and proclaim the good news of life.

But this finger of grace also points us to places we'd rather not go. We who are called to service must be aware that at times we will extend a hand to others and they will reject us. Or even worse, they may pound in a nail or two. But when we open our hands in love for another, though the hammer of rejection may strike a severe blow, may cause a throbbing in our fingers and a piercing of our heart, our commitment to be ministers of God's grace will not be shaken.

We are aware that this precious earth of ours is a garden of good and evil. In these moments of truth when we find our place and God's grace in our own experiences of suffering, rejection and loss, we will be able to offer another a handful of hope. As uncomfortable as this place may be for us, we will offer another some comfort. By our willingness to sit or stand with them in this difficult and dangerous place that has become our lives, we will use our finger and point out that no matter how dry the landscape of the heart may be, something will still grow there. We point to this garden of good and evil and believe that some new hope will grow in this garden. New life will rise from this garden. A new creation will flourish in this garden.

And it has nothing to do with luck. It's all about grace.

Ring Finger: Widening the Circle of Respect

The fourth finger of grace is what we might call our "ring" finger. With this fourth finger we draw a ring of respect around everyone we meet. It is the nature of grace to help us find our common ground.

Sometimes what we know can keep us apart or set us over or against others. Sometimes our differences can keep us apart. But when we recognize, reverence and respect the dignity and dreams of the other, when we choose to see the grace rather than the disgrace that is present in the other, we find our way to each other.

When I think of people I've met along this odyssey of life who spend their lives creating safe spaces — especially in out-of-the-way places — where others can find some common ground and reclaim their dignity and their dreams, I especially think of Depaul Genska. On the day I arrived at Catholic Theological Union (CTU) in Chicago in September, 1978, I met this Franciscan friar who was beginning a sabbatical year. Twenty-three years later, Depaul is still at CTU. The reason why he never left is reflected in the story he told me the first day we met.

Depaul was on staff at a Franciscan retreat house in northern New Jersey that was on the verge of closing. He admitted that he was more than a little naive about the ways of the world, which was reflected in the way he dressed: He wore plaid shirts and striped pants that didn't quite cover his ankles. It is safe to say that Depaul was not a "slave to fashion." His wardrobe seemed to come from the bargain bin at the thrift store. His appearance reflected his Franciscan vow of poverty. Since he often wore the brown habit of his community, he couldn't care less about color coordination. Depaul was more interested in living a faith statement than making a fashion statement.

Late one night in June of 1972, Depaul was driving on a city street when he noticed two young women standing under a street light. He thought they had missed their bus and were stranded in what he considered a dangerous neighborhood. So he stopped his car and offered them a ride. The two women got in the car and looked over this middle-aged man wearing a plaid shirt and striped pants and asked for the money up front. Since they were not brandishing a weapon, Depaul didn't know what they meant. So he asked them where they wanted him to take them. "That's up to you," one of the women said. "But we need the money up front."

It took a while, but it finally dawned on Depaul that these two women were prostitutes. So he took them to a Dunkin' Donuts, bought them coffee and asked them to share their stories about life on the street. That night changed Depaul's life. The women told him how they got involved in prostitution, how they felt trapped and wanted to get out. After hearing their stories that night, Depaul started a ministry to and with prostitutes to help them get out of the world's oldest profession.

Depaul came to Chicago to study at CTU for a year's sabbatical, anticipating that he would return to New Jersey to continue his ministry. Instead, he started a new ministry in Chicago and helped found Genesis House, a sanctuary for women trying to leave prostitution. He works with CTU faculty members to offer a course on street ministry, taking seminarians and students into the streets with him, going to the bars, meeting the people and listening to their stories.

I'm sure he has taken more than his fair share of criticism because, well, it's not exactly the kind of ministry in which any self-respecting Franciscan priest should be involved. He goes to the places where the prostitutes are: to the bars and street corners and red light districts of Chicago. He goes to listen to their stories, to try to show them a way off the street, to try to help them recover their dignity and restore their dreams.

With his ring finger of grace, DePaul Genska draws a ring of respect around all the people he meets. He doesn't wait for them to come to him. He goes looking for them in places few of us would dare to go. In drawing this ring of respect around others, I think of Jesus when the Pharisees tried to set him up by bringing before him a woman caught in the act of adultery, asking Jesus for his opinion in the case (John 8: 1-11). Rather than rendering a verdict in the case, "Jesus bent down and wrote on the ground with his finger" (8: 8). They continued to pester him and tried to trap him. So Jesus, instead of pointing his finger to blame the woman, used his finger to cut through the trap of the religious authorities. He said, "Let the one who is without sin among you be the first to throw a stone at her." Then "once more he bent down and wrote with his finger on the ground" (8: 7).

The stones fell from the peoples' hands. They walked away frustrated that once again Jesus had seen through their trickery. When he finished writing on the ground, he stood up and found himself alone with the woman. He asked her, "Has no one condemned you?" And when she told him, "No," he said, "Neither do I condemn you; go, and do not sin again" (8: 10-11).

The story of Jesus and the woman caught in adultery is just one of many examples the Gospels use to trace the tender mercy of Jesus that reflects the grace of God. For Christians, Jesus is the incarnation of God's mercy. Like Jesus and like DePaul Genska, grace compels us to be on a mission of mercy by drawing a ring of respect around every human being, the innocent and the guilty as well. In doing this, we embrace the ancient truth that Jesus tells the Pharisees in Matthew's Gospel: "It is mercy I desire, not sacrifice" (9: 13).

Jesus was often in hot water with the scribes and Pharisees because he sat at table with known sinners and people who were outside the law. A prime example is when Jesus calls Matthew, a tax collector, to be one of his disciples. After receiving the Master's invitation, Matthew, in turn, invites Jesus to his home to dine. Matthew is throwing himself a going-away party, and so naturally he gathers all those people with whom he has hung around during his career as a tax collector. Now, we know that tax collectors were despised because they extorted their own people to pay off the Romans who were occupying the land. Matthew had sided with the enemy, with the oppressors, and so he was considered a traitor to his people. In the view of the religious leaders, no self-respecting rabbi would ever entertain accepting an invitation to Matthew's den of iniquity.

As Jesus is dining in a den of thieves, the religious authorities raise the question to his disciples, "Why does your teacher eat with tax collectors and sinners?" (Matthew 9: 11). Jesus knows what they are thinking and responds quickly. He uses the metaphor of the doctor-patient relationship, saying healthy people don't need a doctor; sick people do. Then Jesus frames his response in the context of the tradition with which the religious scholars and students of the law would be familiar. He quotes the phrase from Hosea that highlights all of the prophet's teaching: "It is mercy I desire, not sacrifice" (Hosea 6: 6).

Jesus places the dignity of the human person above the unwritten rules about where rabbis should go or not go. He places the extraordinary value of reconciliation in human relationships above the ordinary observance of the law. Jesus focuses on the heart of the individual rather than on the external conformity to rules and regulations. As we see and hear so often, Jesus is on a mission of mercy to those who stand outside the lines of social and religious acceptability. In doing so, he gets under the skin of the religious rule-keepers who don't think they need a doctor but don't know how sick they really are.

Inspired by God's grace, with our ring finger of respect and reverence for every human being, we draw on our common ground a vision of a new heaven and a new earth where all are welcome and all find a place at the table of God's grace.

Rule of Thumb: A Sign of Peace

This brings us to the fifth finger of this hands-on approach to grace: the rule of thumb, which is a sign of peace. When we offer another a hand, we show our desire to get along with the other. In the Roman Catholic tradition, the sign of peace is often expressed by shaking the hands of others before coming forward to receive Communion.

Shaking hands with another is also a sign of welcome and hospitality. Yet it's safe to say that after the death of Jesus the disciples were not a welcoming community. In John's version of the Easter experience, after Mary has told them she has seen the Risen One in the garden, the disciples still lock the doors of the place where they were hiding (John 20: 19-29). But Jesus enters the locked room where the disciples are hidden and says, "Peace be with you" (20: 19).

Jesus brings peace. These are the words he speaks when he appears to his disciples: "Peace be with you." Remember how in John's Gospel, during Jesus' last discourse at the table on the night before he died, he said to them, "Peace is my farewell to you; my peace is my gift to you; I do not give it to you as the world gives peace. Do not be distressed or fearful" (John 14: 27). So peace is the connection. Peace is the way. When he gives them peace after the resurrection, "he showed them his hands and his side" (20: 20). This is the ultimate and most intimate sign of peace: scarred hands and an open side. Then he says to them again, "Peace be with you" (20: 21).

Jesus, the Risen One, is recognized through his wounds. This is how the disciples came to believe in the resurrection: through the wounds of Christ. The welcome sign, the sign that says, "Peace to all who enter here," this sign of peace that reflects the presence of the crucified and risen Jesus in our midst, is visible through our wounds. When we welcome others through our wounds, we invite them into our common story.

But these wounds are more than a calling card, a means of identifying the crucified and risen Jesus. They are also a commission, an invitation to mission. "As the Father has sent me, so I send you" (20: 21). These wounds are the reason we are ministers of reconciliation in the world. The wounded, resurrected Christ breathes upon his disciples and says, "Receive the Holy Spirit. Whose sins you forgive are forgiven them, and whose sins you retain are retained" (20: 22-23).

To receive this commissioning to be ministers of reconciliation, to be a reconciling community that reflects an open door and a sign of peace, we must show up. Thomas was absent. We don't know where he was. Maybe he had errands to run, people to see and miles to go before he could grieve. Or maybe he wasn't afraid like the others locked behind those closed doors. Maybe Thomas didn't care if people recognized him as one of the rabbi's followers. Maybe that upper room was closing in on him and he needed to get some air. Who knows why Thomas wasn't present when Jesus appeared, but we do know that when the others told him, "We have seen the Lord" (20: 25) Thomas wouldn't believe it.

Not until he touched the wounds on the body of Christ.

For a week, the Gospel says, Thomas was an unbeliever. He could not, would not, believe that Christ had risen from the dead. But in his doubt Thomas did recognize one important thing: He knew the resurrected body of Jesus would not be perfect. He knew that even if this rising were true, the skin of Jesus would not be silky smooth but rather would bear the marks of his suffering and death. Doubting Thomas' intuition told him the wounds would be visible on the body of Christ.

Then, seven days of doubt later, Jesus comes again. The doors are still locked. Becoming a welcoming, reconciling community doesn't happen overnight, or over a weekend, or even over the span of seven days and nights. Jesus goes directly to Thomas and says, "Put your finger here and see my hands, and bring your hand and put it in my side" (20: 27). Thomas, the daring yet doubting one, the absent and agnostic one, utters the absolute statement of faith: "My Lord and my God" (20: 28).

With this, Thomas and the other disciples become a welcoming community in the crucified and risen Christ. This is the rule of thumb of how we become a sign of peace to others: through the wounds of Christ. We become a reconciling community where others can find a safe and sacred place to believe in the real presence of the crucified and resurrected Jesus through our wounds.

After his resurrection, Jesus took a "hands-on" approach in convincing his disciples that he has was truly risen from the dead. As we journey in faith during this grace odyssey, the work of our hands is to continue to bear witnesses to the resurrection of Jesus by being a reconciling, welcoming community of faith. The welcome sign of peace hangs on the unlocked door of our heart. We provide a safe place for one another and for all by not being afraid to show our wounds. We are a wounded but redeemed community of faith. The Body of Christ we call the Church is wounded, but we bear witness to the resurrection of Jesus by not being afraid to breathe and believe in new life.

In ancient Assyria the word for prayer literally meant, "to open the fist." When we open our hands, we are taking a position of prayer. We are not afraid to show our wounds. And when we place our hands in the side of the crucified and risen Christ, we no longer take sides. When we reach inside the body of Christ, wash our hands and hopes in the water and blood that flows from his side, our differences are washed away in the redeeming stream of God's grace. We don't need to take sides. The side of Jesus says, "God is on our side."

We are a reconciling and welcoming community when we reflect to the larger church and to the world that the peace of Christ comes through the wounds on the Body of Christ. Through those wounds, all are welcome. In our wounds, all find a safe place to breathe, to believe and to become a people redeemed in the blood of Christ.

Compassion is our rule of thumb. If we are not compassionate with one another, with those we serve, then we can be sure of this: There is no spirituality evident here; there is no community being created here. Perhaps our main task is to act with a quality of compassion that will restore others to wholeness. The question we must continually ask ourselves is: Does my service awaken others to the power of the divine presence among us? Compassion implies a willingness to suffer with and for others. It's not suffering just for the sake of suffering — that would be insanity. It involves suffering with others because in our shared sorrow we will find the key to our identity as compassionate people. But this compassion begins first with ourselves. If we are to be a compassionate presence with and among others, it begins with being compassionate toward our own wounds.

A Map of Our World: In the Palm of Our Hand

I imagine that most of us have very little time on our hands. I suspect that using our hands to juggle so many different responsibilities, we wonder if we're making much of a dent or a difference in the world. We "throw up our hands" in frustration.

One way to get a handle on this experience — and to handle it with care — is to map out the territory of our lives. The map is in our hands — in the palm of our hands. As that eccentric old man asked Patch Adams, "How many fingers do you see?" to help him gain a new perspective on his life, look closely at your hands. See this as a "hands-on" activity, a ten-finger approach to compassionate presence.

When we look at our hands, the whorls of our fingertips, what do we see? Do we grasp how unique each of us truly is? Do we understand how these hands, these fingers, can allow the power of love, the power of God, to flow through to touch another with healing? Do we sense the energy that flows from a heart of integrity because these hearts of ours are focused and fixed on God's compassion welling up inside of us?

Do we sense the power we hold in the palm of our hands? This power is not our own, of course, but it's a power that flows through us because of our belief in God's compassionate presence. We can use the fingers of our hands to point out another's faults and failures, or we can use them to point to the good that is within them. We can use these fingers to write words of criticism or condemnation, or to write words of affirmation and encouragement to those who need to hear them. We use these fingers, these hands, to build up or to tear down.

We can wrap these fingers around our palm to clench a fist, or we can open these hands to extend a sign of peace. We can use these hands to slap another's face in an act of violence, or we can slap another on the back as a sign of congratulations. We can use these hands to grab hold of a grudge, or we can embrace with mercy and forgiveness the one who has hurt us.

The assessment for the work of grace, the work of our hands, is very simple and very sacred. At the end of the day, when dusk settles upon the land and the work of the day is complete, we can look at our hands and ask two questions: What fingerprints have I left behind this day on another's soul, another's life? Whose fingerprints are etched upon my heart?

Psalm: The Hands of Time

I have no idea what time it is.
The power is off; my watch has stopped.
For once I am free to resist the hands of time
pushing me, prodding me, patronizing me.

Time's hands are strong enough to hold me,
gentle enough to caress me,
callused enough to show me courage,
tender enough to teach me compassion.

The hands of time teach me wisdom,
the wisdom to hide in pockets of silence
and listen to the snow falling in the forest now and then
before working my fingers to the bone again.

Chapter Nine

Signature of the Soul: Leaving Our Mark by Taking Care

Ah, the beauty of being at peace with another,
neither having to weigh thoughts or measure words,
but spilling them out just as they are,
chaff and grain together,
certain that a faithful hand will keep what is worth keeping,
and with a breath of kindness blow the rest away.
—Arab proverb

Like the uniqueness of our fingerprints, each of us has what C.S. Lewis called "the secret signature of the soul." That is, each of us leaves a mark on this world and on other human beings by virtue of our identity. The "what" we do that flows out of the "who" we are begins with the self-revelation in our soul that we are uniquely gifted.

We discover meaning in life when we look for the secret signature on our souls. As we reflected in the last chapter, one's unique call is captured in one's thumbprint. Each of us leaves our fingerprints on the work that we do. But one's signature also captures one's unique identity. No one has a signature quite like yours. Some may try to copy it or forge your signature, but they will never duplicate it perfectly.

Hidden in the swirls and curls and scribbles of our signature is the truth of our lives. Now, I am not a handwriting analyst. There are workshops and retreats given just for this purpose — to find one's meaning and truth in the way one writes. But what I'm suggesting here is that because of God's grace, each of us is gifted. Just as our signature says something unique about us, so too do our gifts. Though our gifts may share many aspects in common with others, no two person's gifts are exactly alike. Even for those who cannot read or write and use an "X" to sign their name, if the mark is made by their hand then it is singularly their own.

The signature line I often use when I conclude a letter is "Take good care — may we meet often in prayer and linger there awhile." I remember the old Sarge character in the television show *Hill Street Blues* always telling his police troops at the end of their morning meeting and before they hit the street, "Let's be careful out there." Care is also the signature in Matthew's judgment of the good and the bad — the sheep and the goats (Matthew 25: 31-46). We see that in the signature line: Did you care for each other? Were you caretakers of God's kindom? Or were you careless?

The grace of God that comes to us through Christ is manifested in the care we share with one another. As we suggested in the last chapter, grace is a "hands-on" kind of experience. We are to take care not only of ourselves but of one another, especially those who are most in need. Matthew lists those who are most in need: the hungry, the thirsty, the sick, the imprisoned, the naked and the dead.

Notice that Matthew's "care package" does not mention going to church or fulfilling one's liturgical obligation as signature items that will help us make the waiting list of heaven. This is not to say that prayer is not important. Prayer is the "hands-up" experience of surrender before God. This is what we do when we surrender, isn't it? We put our "hands up." The palms of our hands are open to receive the grace and mercy of God.

But mercy is the common ingredient in all the activities listed in Matthew's care package. They are the "corporal works of mercy," which reflect the presence of God's grace.

Forgiving the Debts

Our signatures also carry a certain amount of weight. For example, when we "sign off" on something or someone, we say it's okay. "Signing off" is different from "writing off" someone. When we sign off on something we give our permission. When we sign a check or sign a letter or sign a document, we put our lives on the line. And I mean this quite literally: We sign our lives away.

The Christian story says that when God became human in the person of Jesus he signed his life away for the forgiveness of sin. He signed his name in blood, on a cross. In doing so, mercy became God's signature line. God writes off our debts. Likewise, what God desires most of us is that we be merciful to one another.

When someone has hurt our feelings or bruised us in some way, we may say, "He owes me an apology." Our forgiveness of the other depends on the other's willingness to apologize. This is a debt. The other owes us.

But God writes off the debt. Our debt of sin is paid in full. We don't owe God anything.

And we owe God everything.

God does not demand an apology before God forgives. God is not so small that God believes we have to get down on our knees and beg forgiveness and apologize before God grants pardon and writes off our debts. If we think in this manner, we are making God into our image and likeness. God doesn't demand an apology. Rather, God inspires a life of grace that gives us the courage to apologize and accept another's apology.

God writes off all debts through the blood of Jesus. No apologies are necessary.

But if we want to apologize, there is no doubt that the apology will be accepted.

Twenty years ago, Catherine Ryan Hyde, the author of *Pay It Forward*, a book that became a movie that became a movement, was driving home one night when her car started to spew sparks and smoke. She came to a screeching halt and jumped out of the car. Suddenly she saw two men running toward her with a blanket. Since this was a rather infamous part of Los Angeles known more for its muggings than its works of mercy, Catherine thought she was about to be assaulted. Instead, these two men with the blanket smothered the fire in her car.

When she regained her composure, Catherine wanted to thank them but they were gone. She wanted to pay them back for the courage they showed in putting out the fire in her car, but they left the scene of their compassion too quickly. So, since she didn't know who these two men were and, thus, couldn't pay back their kindness, she decided to "pay it forward." This experience became the basis for her novel and then a movie in the summer of 2000. It also became the basis for a movement that needs to grow in our world. When we have experienced the kindness of others, instead of trying to pay them back we pass on this compassion and kindness to someone else. We pay it forward.

On this odyssey of grace, when we experience the favor of God's forgiveness and our disgrace is erased in a pool of divine pardon and peace, we are invited to pray the forgiveness we experience forward to someone else. This is how we might pray it forward: by extending the mercy we receive to someone who owes us an apology. Instead of demanding the debt be paid, because God writes off all the debts caused by our sin, we write off the debts of those who owe us an apology. We pray forward the pardon and peace we receive by forgiving those who have hurt us or harmed us, betrayed us or belittled us.

If we have received the forgiveness of someone else, if someone we owed an apology has forgiven our trespass, then we can pray that forward too. We don't look back — we always look forward. This is what hope does: It is always forward looking. The virtue of hope doesn't dwell on the past but looks to the future. We pray hope forward when we acknowledge all that God has done for us in the past and is doing for us in the present as we look forward to the future.

When we sin, God doesn't demand an apology. All God asks is that we pray the pardon and peace we receive forward to someone else in our lives who needs our mercy. Pray for that person in our lives who desires our forgiveness. Pray for that person in our lives we find most difficult to love. Pray for that person who is on the brink of despair. Pray for those people in our lives — those strangers and family and friends — who have helped us in the past, those we'd love to pay back but can't. So in their name, in their memory, we pray their kindness forward to someone else.

This is how hope becomes more than a virtue; it becomes our victory. We pray the promise forward. We pray the hope forward. We pray forgiveness forward — to that one who most needs to receive our pardon and our peace.

The Cost of Living: Forgiving

Like paying a kindness forward, praying forgiveness forward doesn't come without a cost. Recently I heard that the cost of living goes up about 4% each year. Each year it costs more to live. It is built into budget and salary increases. It is a fact of life. Like death and taxes, it is a fact that it costs more to live each year.

In the spiritual life, the cost of living increases also. This is the high cost of living: forgiving. If we live long enough, there will be more than enough people to forgive. To live without regret seems more difficult to do than to live without modern conveniences like microwaves, cell phones or VCRs. How did we live without them? Of course, regret is not a convenience. It certainly doesn't make life easier. But regret is a fact of life.

If we live long enough, we have to learn — or reclaim the innate ability of children — to forgive, because we inevitably experience hurt and harm at the hands of another. It may not be a physical attack. It may be the voice of another that attacks, when a person's words become like bullets that cause our soul to bleed. Or another may turn a deaf ear to our cries for help, and the scar caused by indifference becomes permanently etched upon our souls. When others have hurt us, our soul is marked. Often, such tattoos are not easily removed; a scar usually survives.

We can cut our losses, but this won't keep the cost of living from going up. We can forgive our debts and the debts others have on the ledger sheet of our lives. But this only goes to prove that the cost of living is forgiving — and it increases every year.

During this grace odyssey, whose debts do we need to write off? What debts that others have incurred against us do we need to sign off on? And why in the world — in this world or the next — are we waiting to forgive?

Perhaps one of the reasons we find it difficult to forgive is that if we wait too long to forgive someone who has hurt us, the hurt becomes hard. When others become aware that they have hurt us, they may say, "No hard feelings." Even though our feelings are hurt, we promise our hurt will not grow hard. But over time, the hurt often hardens. This is what happens to unresolved hurt — it grows hard. When our feelings have been hurt and we fail to address them honestly — fail to name them and claim them as hurt — then we may not even realize how these old hurts harden our hearts.

The prospect of such progressive hardening forces us to face the cost of living. It confronts us with a choice: to forgive or not to forgive. We can let go of old hurts and soften our hard hearts, or we can cling to those old hurts until they become so hard that when the person who first inflicted the hurt asks for forgiveness, we choose to ignore the request. We can choose healing or to keep on hurting. We can choose to open our minds or slam them shut, keep our hearts moist or make them hard.

But if we wait too long to forgive, we shouldn't be surprised if when the hurt hardens we find it hard to forgive — and also find the riverbeds of life drying up and hardening within us.

Check the Timing Belt

This is why, in the process of pardoning, timing is everything. Here is another image that may help us get at the truth of why forgiveness is so difficult.

I know very little about cars. I know where to put in the gas and how to check, but not change, the oil. When I need an oil change — every 3,000 miles I was told by an expert — I take it to one of those places that promises to change the oil and give the car a physical in thirty minutes or less. I trust they are not only fast and friendly but competent. I trust that when I turn the key the engine will respond. There, that's my expertise regarding automobiles.

A few years ago I was discussing my car with a friend who knows a lot more about the inner workings of an automobile than I do. When I told him I had 75,000 miles on the car, he suggested I get the belts changed. Especially the timing belt, he said, because if that breaks the car just stops. Well, I followed my friend's advice. First, though, I consulted the owner's manual for the car — a book I consult about as often as I peruse the Code of Canon Law — and, sure enough, the factory recommendation was to change the timing belt every 60,000 miles. I was 15,000 miles overdue.

I took the car into an auto repair place where many of the members of my community have taken their cars over the years. I told them to change all the belts. "Including the timing belt?" the man behind the counter asked. "Oh, yes," I said, pretending I knew how crucial this belt was. "I'm running on borrowed time with that timing belt."

The mechanic kept the car all day, and when I returned in the evening to pick up the car, I was handed the bill. "There must be some mistake!" I screamed at the man behind the counter. "How can this bill be so much?" Before he responded, I added with a sarcasm usually reserved only for people I know well, "What kind of belts did you put on my car — gold-plated ones?"

The guy behind the counter explained that the timing belt was the major expense.

"How can that be?" I asked in a flurry of fury.

He explained that the belt itself isn't very expensive but that it's difficult to get to. The mechanic has to take the engine apart. "It's very labor intensive," he said.

"You mean labor *expensive*," I replied.

I couldn't comprehend how a $2.00 belt costs $400.00 to replace. Well, that might be a slight exaggeration, but at any rate I learned something about timing belts that day.

On this grace odyssey in the new millennium, as we try to pace ourselves in the wide-open spaces of a new century, we need to check our timing belts. But beware: If we're going to change the belt, we need to be prepared to pay a steep price. Again, this is the high cost of living and forgiving. We can risk continuing this grace odyssey without replacing the timing belt, but we should be aware that if the belt breaks, our soul will stall. So, regular maintenance is important.

The timing belt under the hood of our soul doesn't have anything to do with being punctual. Rather, it has to do with being passionate. We all know people who have a reputation for never showing up on time. Their inner clocks work differently — they always run a little late. But the soul's timing belt doesn't regulate punctuality; it inspires passion.

Some people have an inner sense, an innate sense, of timing. Others of us are often in a hurry, yet we usually know when the time is right. But if our timing belt breaks, our soul stalls. That is why people with a good sense of timing regularly have their belts checked. They follow daily spiritual practices of prayer and meditation that keep their sense of timing intact. They will not allow the pace of the day to determine their schedule or to dictate how much time they will spend in prayer. They know that without proper prayer maintenance, their mission will stall. Solitude and prayer help us to check the timing belt of our lives, to make connections we don't see when the busyness of life is the order of the day.

People of Letters: A Matter of Timing

Maybe we're just waiting for the right time to forgive. Maybe it's a matter of timing. We've heard the excuse, maybe even used it now and then. When we're expecting something important — a birthday card, a check, a government form — we sometimes hear, "It's in the mail." It may be late or not in the time frame we anticipated, but "it's in the mail."

We might look at that familiar phrase not as an excuse but an invitation to keep our sacred connections running (or walking) smoothly — and a way to practice graceful living. It's an invitation to a spiritual exercise about our sense of timing. One way we strengthen our sense of timing is through the ancient art of writing a letter.

A mailbox with the flag up indicates to the mail carrier that there is a letter waiting to be picked up. A religious sister once told me how important that mailbox became for her. Both of her parents are dead. Her mother died first. Her father lived for several years after his wife died. When she went to his house after his funeral to pack some things and get the house ready for sale, one of the things she took with her was the mailbox. She did this, she told me, because one of her favorite images of her dad after her mom died was how he would wait each day for the mail to be delivered. He would especially welcome a letter from her, his only daughter. And he would immediately write back to her that night and put the letter in the mailbox with the flag up.

In this age of fast-paced, almost instant, communication, traditional mailboxes are quickly becoming storage sheds for junk. And bills. And magazines that no one has time to read because we are answering our E-mail. Still, a flag up on the mailbox is a signal for the letter carrier to stop, even if he only has a bill you'd rather not receive or junk mail that will be taken from one box and thrown immediately into another container. Looking out the window and seeing the flag is down, hope flutters in one's heart. There may be a letter from home.

There is a time to write letters and a time to receive them. Waiting for letters from home when we are away for an extended period is one of the time frames I most recall when I was in the seminary. Every day after lunch we gathered in study hall and listened for the sound of our names as the mail was distributed. When we heard our name, we took the letter and took our time reading every word, savoring every page.

Who needs to hear from us? Who needs to receive a letter that is signed by our own hand and which says, "All is forgiven"?

When thinking about writing such a letter, remember what the mechanic who changed the timing belt on my car told me: It's the location of the belt that makes the job "labor expensive." The timing belt is located in a place where the mechanic has to take the engine apart in order to change the belt.

The location of the timing belt suggests that to strengthen the sacred connection with those we love it does make a difference where our words come from. Do our words come from the "bottom of our heart" or "off the top of our head?" When we've thought about something for a long time — an apology or words of gratitude or sentiments of consolation or sympathy — we are likely to write or speak from the bottom of our heart. For some, this phrase has become a cliche. For me, it reflects a certain truth that the person who is writing or speaking has taken the time to plumb the depths — a place that, in the words of my mechanic friend, is "difficult to get to" — in order to find just the right words.

It'is like the host going down to the wine cellar to choose just the right wine for a dinner party. The person's words that come from the bottom of the heart have been aging a while. Only after the right amount of time in the wine cellar of the soul are the words ready to be served.

When we speak "off the top of our heads," we admit that not much thought or study or consideration has gone into what is about to be said. Someone asks a question, and we pause for just a moment. We preface our answer with, "off the top of my head." It's just a thought, an idea, maybe even an insight, but it is stored at the top of our heads and not at the bottom of our hearts.

So what kinds of information do we store at the top of our heads? What meaning or memories are so close to the surface that they are easily released at random when we are asked a question? Sometimes we say, "Let me think about that," which implies our response is not carried in the inventory stored at the top of our head. We have to go deeper. Maybe even to the bottom of our heart.

Or down to the wine cellar of our soul.

If someone has been invited to speak to a group, it is expected that what the person is going to say is from the stash in the bottom of his or her heart. Or the message could come from the person's ever-expanding library of the mind, or even, depending upon the topic, fine wine from the cellar of the soul, and not just off the top of his or her head. The person who has been given ample time to prepare normally doesn't speak "off the cuff." That's another interesting turn of a phrase that originated with speakers writing notes on the cuffs of their white shirts so they wouldn't forget. We have taken "off the cuff" remarks to mean spontaneous and unrehearsed comments — like those that come off the top of our heads. But taking the time to write one's remarks on the cuffs of one's clothes implies a certain preparation. Still, we must be careful because the speaker who talks "off the cuff" may have something "up his or her sleeve."

Of course, one who is well prepared doesn't necessarily find all the material for a presentation in the bottom of one's heart. It could come "out of one's mind," but then that carries a different meaning. We've probably been to presentations where we thought the speaker was out of his or her mind! If the word comes out of one's mind rather than the bottom of one's heart, it may be very factual, but it's not likely to be very passionate. In the bottom of the heart there are sentiments and emotions, scars and stories that evoke deep meanings that can be moving. Besides raising our ideas to the level of what poet Samuel Taylor Coleridge called "felt thought," emotion can move us. We don't want to stay in the same place. E-mail may be convenient, but "E-motion" moves us to compassion.

And when we hear something that is "gut-wrenching," well, we know the origin from which the speaker speaks: It comes from the place we call the soul.

Reclaiming a Lost Art

Writing letters is quickly becoming a lost art. Maybe it has something to do with the price of a first class stamp. But I suspect the real cost of letter writing is determined not so much by postal rates as by how much time it takes to write a letter. Writing a letter in pen and ink, in longhand, without using a typewriter or a computer is time-consuming.

Composing a letter, like composing a life, takes time.

With the advent of E-mail, we can communicate quickly, efficiently and less expensively. My computer beeps and a voice says, "You've got mail" when I have E-mail waiting for me to read. Since the inception of E-mail, there are those who suggest we are more connected than ever before. With no envelope to address or to seal and no stamps to affix, E-mail is certainly easier than regular or, as some like to call it, "snail mail." E-mail addresses are exchanged as frequently as phone numbers. Some even say that while E-mail seems impersonal, people often get very personal in their E-mail correspondence since thoughts seem to stream as quickly as one can type. Punctuation is not an issue since commas and periods only slow one down and the emphasis of E-mail is efficiency and speed. The lack of capitalization is not a capital offense. The rules of grammar meet the rules of the road and fly out the window on the information highway, where there is no speed limit.

I guess it's true that E-mail keeps us connected to those people we might not correspond with otherwise, but it also seems that while we may be more connected in cyberspace, we are losing touch with a sacred space. It's the touch of holding in our hands a handwritten letter from a friend or family member. Holding that letter with a reverence reserved for a sacred species and reading the words written, not typed, by the hand of another affords a kind of intimacy that nourishes the soul. It takes time to write a letter, to put one's thoughts and feelings on paper. It's much easier to E-mail a letter, but a certain intimacy is lost when using the express lane on the information highway. If all we're looking for is information, then E-mail is fine. But if we want to live gracefully in time and space, if we are searching for a holy intimacy, a sacred connection, with other human beings, then a handwritten letter is still the best avenue of communication.

There's something graceful and comforting about the feel of stationery and seeing words etched in a person's unique handwriting. There is magic in this method of communication. For me, it has to do with time. It's all in the timing. The other has taken time from a busy life to think only of me — to tell a little bit of the story of what's happening in his or her life. The person has taken the time to write. It is a gift. It deserves a response. The flag on the mailbox is up. Longhand lines of communication and conversation of a sacred kind are now open.

Of course, not everyone has penmanship that is legible. Imagine writing words of pardon to a person and he or she not being able to read it because our handwriting seems to resemble an ancient script found on stones in Egyptian archaeological digs! Bad penmanship is not only difficult to read, it can also be dangerous. Recently I heard of a remedial school in California where doctors go to improve their handwriting. It seems that because some doctors have such poor handwriting when they write prescriptions, pharmacists have given the wrong medicine.

According to handwriting experts who are able to tell much about someone's personality by analyzing the person's handwriting, there are twelve principles of good penmanship: form, slant, spacing, margins, neatness, organization, arrangement, balance, fluency, judgment, precision and accuracy. In looking over that list, some of these principles might apply to this grace odyssey, like the need for *spacing*, *balance* and *right judgment* (one of the gifts of the Holy Spirit). But for the most part the spiritual journey takes many *forms*, is given to many *slants*, often exists outside the *margins*, is rarely *neat* and suffers at times from a lack of *organization*. The spiritual odyssey is *arranged* differently according to the gifts and needs of each seeker, is *fluent* in various languages, and often lacks *precision*. Perhaps the most *accurate* application of the principles of good penmanship to the principles of spiritual companionship is that each of our journeys is as unique as our handwriting.

A Sacred Connection

When we write cursively, there is an interconnection between letters. Writing a letter to a friend also reflects the sacred connection of relationship. The Christian Scriptures contain numerous letters that reflect this desire for holy connection. Some of these letters are credited to the three apostles often mentioned in the Gospels as close associates of Jesus: Peter, James and John. But by far the majority of the letters in the Christian Scriptures are attributed to Paul, who is writing to new communities in ancient places like Rome, Corinth, Ephesus and Philippi. There are also some of Paul's letters that are written to individuals, like Timothy, Titus and Philemon.

Paul's second letter to Timothy reflects a quality of intimacy and graciousness that is at the heart of the lost art of letter writing. I can imagine Timothy's eyes lighting up when he is told, "You have mail." It is another letter from his teacher, Paul. His words are written with care and with love for his young friend. This is a letter to a young missionary from his mentor, who at the time is in prison. Paul writes not only to show his support for his protégé, whom he calls "my dear child whom I love" (2 Timothy 1: 2), but to challenge him. Evidently, Timothy is being timid in giving witness. Paul reminds him "to stir into flame the gift God bestowed when my hands were laid on you" (2 Timothy 1: 6). This gift of the Spirit, Paul writes, "is no cowardly spirit but rather one that makes us strong, loving and wise." Paul's letter offers encouragement to Timothy in a time when his young friend is fearful and weak.

It probably took a long time for Paul's letter to reach Timothy, but when it arrived, can you not imagine Timothy holding this letter in his hands, reading Paul's handwriting and finding courage welling up in his fearful heart? Can you not sense Timothy's heart beginning to burn with passion again even as Paul writes of the "hardship which the Gospel entails" (1: 8)? Yes, this letter probably took a long time to reach Timothy, and yet it is really a kind of "air mail" because Paul is breathing some fresh air into Timothy's timid life.

I suspect we have had similar experiences: We're feeling down or feeling out of breath, feeling like the air has been knocked out of us, feeling fearful and fragile. Then the mail arrives, and we check the box and find a letter from a friend who has heard we are going through a difficult time. We hold the letter and read the words, and something begins to burn inside our heart. We find new courage to continue. We discover new hope. We are reminded, as Paul reminds Timothy, that we are called to "a holy life, not because of any merit of ours but according to God's own design" (1: 9). We find in the handwritten words of this friend a gentle breath that blows on dying embers and sparks a flame. The pen of this friend has stirred our faith into flame again.

Such a sacred connection is as close as our fingertips. A pen and a piece of paper are all we need. Our words to a friend are formed not in the head but in the heart. They may be words of condolence or congratulation, words of challenge or comfort. They are words from the pen of one who cares, words the friend reads with gratitude, no matter how long it may take to decipher the handwriting. For the friend knows a letter written in longhand has reached out across the miles with the long arm of a loving embrace.

This is a simple spiritual exercise we can practice each day. The time it takes to write a letter or a note is as important as the words we put on paper. For with each brush of pen against paper, a prayer is etched on parchment. And when the friend reads the letter, the prayer is etched upon his or her heart.

A Record of Relationship

Few words lift our spirit more than someone telling us, "You have mail." In our box, hidden somewhere beneath the magazines and the catalogues and the bills, there is a letter from a friend we haven't heard from in a while. Our spirits, like Timothy's, are lifted as we read the letter slowly, carefully, prayerfully. It is a kind of meditation that moves us to a sacred space, the sanctuary of the heart. The same is true with the friend who receives a note, card or letter from us.

For me, letters like these are not recyclable. I save them because they are simple, sacramental reminders that I am saved, that a friend holds me in his or her heart, is thinking about me and praying with me. I have some letters that are more than thirty years old — letters my mom wrote to me when I was a freshman in high school. I was in the seminary, 250 miles away from home, and those letters from Mom — like Paul's letters to Timothy — breathed some fresh air into my homesick heart. Yes, mail call at the seminary was the high point of each day.

Some may believe that holding on to thirty years' worth of letters entitles me to be a member of the pack rat society. I prefer to think of it as a "record of relationship." Writing a letter is an expression of grace. A thank you note to a friend expresses our gratitude, while a letter to a family member going through a difficult time reflects our compassion. A get well card to someone who is ill is a sign of our care, while a letter of congratulations on someone's accomplishment is a sign of affirmation. A birthday greeting to celebrate the gift of life or a sympathy card to one who has lost a loved one marks the times of our lives and our moments of truth. This is a spiritual activity that reflects a quality of intimacy and of prayer that binds us together, that makes a sacred connection, that reminds the one who receives it that she is loved, that he is not alone.

When we breathe into the envelope a part of our soul, this letter becomes "air mail." Yes, it is slower than E-mail, but it is certainly more soulful and graceful. And who knows, it may just stir into flame a gift of faith or hope or love in the heart of the one who receives the letter. In this consecrated correspondence, this holy communication, the other just might find in our air mail a little more room to breathe.

Who are those people we call our friends who nourish our soul? Take a moment now to reflect with gratitude and hold in prayer those in your life with whom you feel a sacred connection. With a pen, put your prayer to paper and send your friend a letter. In this spiritual exercise it is not necessary to measure your words. Treasure the quality of those beloved ones who through the fidelity and favor of their friendship have made the divine presence real, for these graceful human friendships serve as reflections of our relationship with the holy.

When we spend time in quiet encounters with a true friend, whether in person or through a "love letter," we come to know a bit more about prayer, for in true prayer we neither have to measure our words nor weigh our thoughts because we know the Beloved accepts us as we are. In the gentle presence of a friend, a faithful heart accepts both chaff and grain. A true friend will keep what is worth keeping, and with a gentle breath of kindness blow the rest away.

Psalm: Plenty of Time

Time is like a line
to mark and measure our lives.
Time is a circle
that goes round and round.
Around the clock
we go, and where time stops
nobody knows.

Grant us the grace, O God,
to see that on your time table
there is plenty of time.
This is truly a table of plenty —
plenty of laughter and love,
plenty of forgiveness and faith,
plenty of wine and redemption,
plenty of bread and brokenness.

May we stay at this table of plenty
until we are full —
full of grace,
grace that we might face
the truth:
We are on borrowed time.

We borrow it from you, Divine One,
from your time table of plenty.

Chapter Ten

Time To Go:
The Grace of a Happy Death

Stop the words now.
Open the window in the center of your chest
And let the spirit fly in and out.
—Rumi

We may be living on the edge of eternity,
but that should not make us dismal.
The early Christians rejoiced to think
that the end of the world was near, as they thought.
Are we so unready to face God?
Are we so avid for joys here
that we perceive so darkly those to come?
—Dorothy Day

Living in the present moment is a moment of grace in time. Such living is how time becomes "full of grace" and pregnant with meaning. We have all known people — perhaps we are such people — who are fully present to the moment. What a high compliment it is to pay to another when we say of him or her, "When you speak to her, it's like you are the only person in the world." There are no distractions. There is only a real and grace-filled presence.

If we live in this way, when the hands of time come together at the stroke of midnight and we are told it is time to go, we are ready. This is the ultimate moment of truth, something our spiritual tradition calls "the grace of a happy death." Most of us begin to pray for this grace long before our death, of course. Every time we pray the "Hail Mary," for instance, we ask the Blessed Mother, the one "full of grace," to "pray for us sinners now and at the hour of our death."

So how might we avail ourselves to this grace of a happy death? There is a Hasidic tale about a rabbi who lived an unusually full and gracious life. After his death, one of his disciples was asked, "What was most important to your teacher?" Without hesitating a moment, the student answered, "Whatever he happened to be doing at that moment."

How might we prepare ourselves for this last of the graces we will experience on this side of the Great Divide? The first and most important preparation we can make is to live this present moment as if it was our last and very best moment on earth.

The Wisdom of a Single Day

Once there was a woman who ran a small shop on the town's main street. On one particular day her store was overflowing with customers. In the midst of the mayhem, a friend dropped by to tell her, "Annie, I have great news!"

"This better be important," Annie said with more than a shade of scorn to color her words. "Can't you see how busy I am?"

Her friend winked. "It is important. You once told me you have a burning question within your heart. One that you've shared with no one."

"It's true," Annie said, continuing to work at the counter. "I have yet to find a person with enough wisdom to answer it."

"Well," the friend said, "I've heard of a great saint who lives along the southern coast. Now you have someone who might be able to answer your question."

Annie stared at all her customers. The store was very busy, but she had waited a long time for this. So, she told her customers there had been an emergency and invited them to come back at another time. Annie rushed out the door, got in her car and traveled down the coast to the place where her friend said the saint lived. All the while, the question kept burning deeply in her heart.

After searching for an hour or so, she found herself outside the saint's small seaside hermitage. The door swung open. A small elderly woman stood there smiling at her. "Good morning," she greeted Annie. "Come in, I've been expecting you."

But Annie answered, "I have one question to ask of you, and I'll not move until it's answered."

The saint wiped her hands on her apron, leaned against the open door and waited.

"If you had one day to live — just one day — how would you spend it?"

The old woman gazed out upon the ocean. A breeze brought a few strands of her white hair down upon her face, and she gently brushed them back. "Well," she said softly, "first I would say my morning prayer. Then I'd fix a little coffee and toast. After breakfast, I would go out to weed the garden. Then I would probably go visit my neighbor Gabe since his rheumatism really bothers him this time of year." The old woman paused to watch some gulls dive into the nearby waves.

"After visiting Gabe, I might come back and fix a bite to eat for lunch and then take a short nap."

Annie stopped her. "Wait! I'll bet that's the way you live every day."

The old woman smiled. "Of course. Why would I live my last day any differently?"

How would you answer Annie's question?

The wisdom of the old woman is reminiscent of Jesus' words in the Gospel parable about the wise and foolish servants (Matthew 25: 1-13). Do we live each day of our lives as wise servants who have our lamps ready and waiting for the master to return from the wedding banquet? Are we like that old woman who would live her last day just as any other day because we strive to live each day well?

Wisdom is gained when we keep our eyes open to the beauty of creation and our arms open to embrace the ones we love or the stranger who stands on our porch. Wisdom is gained when we keep our minds open to those with whom we disagree and our hearts open to forgive the one who has hurt us. Though mistakes and missed opportunities may litter the landscape of our lives like so many land mines ready to explode, we don't look back. We don't get bogged down, and we don't allow our past blunders to slow us down. Instead, we live with the attitude that each day offers us occasions of grace to embark on new opportunities of living and loving. We stay alert and awake and ready to move in the motion of God's time, not our own.

Since we don't know the day or the hour of our Master's return — it could be in the middle of the night or closer to sunrise — we watch and wait like "sentinels who wait for the dawn" (Psalm 130: 6) in an active vigil of anticipation. We take this stance not out of fear but because of our faith. We can find no better patron saint for this providential pilgrimage than that old woman who lived by the sea and who lived each day as if it was her last. She knew something about promises that are symbolized by the sands of the seashore: When that sand gets trapped between our toes, we begin to sense something about how our soul needs a walk on the beach every now and then.

That is what we are invited to do each today. On this grace odyssey, we keep moving, with our lamps burning, our stomachs churning, our hearts pumping and our souls on alert. For when Jesus returns, he will usher us in to a banquet hall where a wedding feast has been prepared to celebrate a cosmic, consecrated union of body and soul, mind and spirit.

It takes courage to live each day as if it is our last. It also takes patience. And since God never acts on our clock, it takes time. But if we walk this grace odyssey with hearts open to surprise and eyes open to see God's presence, we will mirror the experience of our ancestors in faith who believed that the Messiah would return and take his place at the Passover. When Jesus did not return right away, the early church celebrated the agape meal as a way to remind themselves that something's always cooking in God's kitchen.

On our pilgrimage of God's providence, may we stop long enough to be reminded of that old woman's gift to Annie in her search for the answer to her question. This is the treasure: to live each day well in the company of friends, with fresh bread and fine wine, and to discover the foretaste and promise of a banquet that will never end.

Spiritual Exercises

We can make ourselves available to the grace of a happy death through certain spiritual exercises. As athletes train and prepare through various drills and warm-ups to get ready for a big game, we can train our hearts and souls to be ready at any moment to be called home. As Bill Moyers' Public Television series *On Dying* reminded us, most of us are afraid to talk about our own dying. Yet we can prepare for this grace of a happy death in a way that is life-giving rather than morbid by affirming how generous God has been to us throughout our lives. Here are some spiritual exercises to help us prepare for the grace of a happy death.

Visit a cemetery. Spend some time on a sunny afternoon reading the "writing on the wall" — the names, the verses, the poetry etched on tombstones. If the graves have pictures of the deceased, pause a moment and study the face. Visit your own family plot and allow the memories of the deceased members of your family to surface in your soul. If you have already purchased a plot, sit down on that holy ground and feel the earth beneath your body. Thank God for the graces and blessings that God has shown you throughout your life.

Hope in the palm of your hand. Trace the lines of God's love in the palm of your hand. Bring to mind with loving gratitude the people — your family, friends, coworkers, mentors and even strangers — who have touched your life with the grace of God. Thank God for the special places where you have lived or worked — those places where you might tell another, "This is where I spent some of the best years of my life." Treasure the vacations you've taken, the retreats you've made, the books you've read, the movies you've seen. Fondly recall the situations or experiences in your life that have been life-giving, graceful, joyful or growthful. Your life is in the palm of your hand! Take a long, loving look at your life and when you do, know you are preparing the ground, making the soil of your soul ready, for the grace of a happy death.

Spend time in a sacred space. Besides a cemetery, there are other places you might visit to consider this grace of a happy death — places where you may experience God's favor. Spend some time at those spaces in your life that you deem "holy ground." What made that ground holy for you? Maybe it is a mountaintop or a meditation garden, a forest in spring or fall or the ocean as summer wanes. Perhaps it is a chapel or church or a cabin deep in the woods in winter as the snow falls.

Write your obituary. When I taught a course on Death and Dying to high school juniors several years ago, two activities — visiting a funeral home and writing a personal obituary — were highlights of the semester. I invited the students to write the truth of their lives. I asked them to see themselves at the end of their lives and to look back at what they did for a living — and for a life. A variation on this theme is to imagine one's wake service and the stories that will be told about you when you die. Those stories are being created each day of our lives. The truth of our lives is found in this simple, spiritual exercise: What stories will be told about us when we die — especially by those we love the most?

Visit the living. Perhaps the best preparation for the grace of a happy death is to visit the person you most need to visit, saying the things you most need to say to the one who needs to hear your words. Don't wait until it's too late. Since we don't know the when or the how or maybe even the why, grace and time come together to remind us that today is the day to prepare to die. Each day we can do something to get the ground of our being ready for the grace of a happy death.

Waiting at the Terminal

When I was giving a retreat in Wisconsin for religious women a few years ago, a sister came to see me privately and said, "I don't want to put any pressure on you, but this will probably be my last retreat on this side of the Great Divide." Though her body reflected what she meant, she went on to explain that she had been engaged in a battle with liver cancer for almost a year. "The disease is terminal," she said as a matter of fact, without a hint of remorse or regret.

Then this woman whose days were numbered smiled and said, "One day a few months ago I saw on my chart that the nurse had written, "Sister denies she is terminal." I wasn't supposed to see that note, but it forced me to look at death in a new way."

I asked her how those words, "Sister denies she's terminal" freed her to embrace death. And she said, "Well, that note could be written on all our charts, couldn't it? Don't we all deny we are terminal? Don't we all live today as if tomorrow is assumed? Don't we all make plans for next week, next month, next year? To some extent we all deny that we're terminal, that we're going to die."

That word *terminal* seems so cold, like a bus stop or a train station or an airport at the end of the world. But as this sister noted, "terminal" is written on all our spiritual charts. Seeing that word may give us the freedom to approach our condition of waiting at the terminal with a sense of hope, maybe even expectation, because we believe our final destination is not death, but life.

Sometimes in life we seem stuck at the terminal with no place to go. Our connecting flight has been delayed. Our trip home has been canceled because of the weather or other conditions out of our control. We do the best we can to pass the time. But the waiting seems endless. The minutes seem to struggle to become hours, and the hours seem to stagger under the weight of our waiting. The clock's face seems to smirk at our predicament, mocking our futile attempts to be patient.

There is a Gospel story that speaks of this mocking face of time. A group known as the Sadducees, who profess there is no resurrection, no afterlife, come to Jesus with a carefully constructed scenario which they believe has "no exit." They do this to try to trap Jesus in his teaching about life after death. The scenario suggested by the Sadducees involves seven brothers for one bride. Each brother, in turn, marries the same woman after the death of the previous brother. In the end, they all have died, leaving the woman a widow. According to Jesus' teaching about the resurrection, in the afterlife, which of the seven brothers would lay claim to the woman as his wife?

Jesus punches their ticket for their final destination by punching a few holes in their scenario about the seven brothers marrying the same woman. Jesus says that people who believe in the resurrection will become like angels and are no longer liable to death. He draws upon the ancient tradition of Moses and evokes the God of their ancestors to point to our past as well as our future and final destination as a place of life instead of death.

In responding to the Sadducees' scenario, Jesus makes the point that eternal life is not simply an extension of this earthly life but rather an entirely new existence. This is not wishful thinking or a flight of fantasy. Our hope in the future does not depend on our own dreams that may or may not come true, but on God's dreams for us.

Because our God is a God of life, not death, God dreams that we experience the fullness of life. God's dream for us is based on an itinerary that shows our destiny is eternity.

A Parable About Eternal Life

When I asked that sister who was waiting at the terminal what had helped her to embrace death as a fact of this life, to see death not as a destination but as a connecting point to an even better destination, she told me a story. I had heard the parable somewhere before, but when it was spoken by someone who was looking squarely into the face of death, the parable took on an even more powerful meaning.

In the manner of the teacher she had been for so many years, the sister asked, "To what can we compare our birth into everlasting life?" Then she told me this parable:

Consider the image of a child in the womb of her mother. Before she is born, the child is safe and secure in her mother's womb. Can we imagine this child thinking, "This is a wonderful place. It's warm and cozy. I am well fed and taken care of. This is a great world where I'm living now. I like it. I want to stay here."

But then a voice says, "But you cannot stay here. You have to move on. You are going to another world."

And what is the child's response to this? When a baby is born, the first thing she does is scream. She cries. She's been taken from the world of the womb to a brand new world. If the child could talk, she might say, "Put me back! I want to stay in the womb!"

What to us is birth, to the child is death, and she resists it. And she might continue to resist this new world if she is not immediately after birth cradled in loving arms. Soft hands hold her gently. A kind face looks down at her, and she loves the face. Everyone who comes to see her, to hold her, looks at her with such joy and love.

Indeed, she is the center of attention. Still she cries. But now she begins to sense that when she cries she gets even more attention. She begins to figure out that when she cries people immediately respond because they want her to be safe and dry and to feel at home in this brand new world.

She begins to grow, and the longer she lives in this world, the more comfortable she becomes. She has some struggles and hardships, of course. She knows difficulties and more than a few sorrows. But overall, this new world is pretty good. With its changing seasons and breathtaking beauty, with its loving relationships and wondrous friends, she likes this world.

But then, after many, many years in this world, she begins to grow older, and a voice says, "You know, one of these days you are going to die." But she protests, "I don't want to die! I like it here! I love this world. I like to feel the sun on my face and the cool rain. I like to be around other people. I love my family and friends. I have lived here a long time. I don't want to die."

But one day she does die. And once again there are tears and fears, for she has left this world she has grown to love and gone to yet another world. She is born yet again. She will awaken to find herself young again. Loving faces long forgotten will greet her. Loving hands will welcome her and touch her. More beautiful sunlight will surround her. Sweeter music than she ever heard in the other world will play in her heart. All her tears will be wiped away. And she will come to the conclusion, "Why was I so afraid of this thing called death, when, as I know now, this is life."

In recalling this parable for me, this woman who was waiting at the terminal, waiting for her connecting flight to everlasting life, was someone who, in the wonderful phrase of Elie Wiesel, was "intoxicated with eternity." While waiting at the terminal, no matter how long the wait, we make good use of the time we have by drinking deeply of life. We may strike up a conversation with a stranger. We may look with kind eyes and a warm smile at the harried ticket agent trying to help impatient passengers find their way home. We may take a walk around the station and just look at the faces. Or we may bury our head in a book or a magazine and take a connecting flight on board our own imagination.

When we become "intoxicated with eternity," we taste all the experiences our life serves us with the patience of one who knows where one is going: home. Sooner or later, this is our destination. We are homeward bound. Bound for an eternal time zone that places all one's life, all one's relationships, all one's experiences in the "now."

Our challenge as we wait at the terminal is to take a drink of life and become intoxicated with eternity. In the words of Tony de Mello, we need to stop "reading the labels," and instead "drink the wine."

Eternity invites us to stop reading the labels — or labeling each other — and to drink deeply of the new wine of compassion, the wine of new life, that we taste in each other's stories.

We do this in the same ways as that sister with the terminal illness told me she did it. We do it by not taking others for granted. We prepare for the grace of a happy death by living each day well, by keeping our eyes and our arms open to receive another's pardon or to give another the gift of peace, by keeping our hearts open to each joy and sorrow that is served up to us. We prepare by taking a nap after lunch if we feel like it — because life is too short not to take a nap when we need one!

That is the sound advice given to me by the religious sister I met waiting at the terminal several years ago. She has gone home now, but I still drink deeply from her story. And the more I do, the more I see lifelines instead of deadlines, the more I become intoxicated with eternity.

The more we view life and death in these terms, seeing death as our connecting flight to everlasting life, the less our waiting at the terminal is to be feared; rather it becomes filled with expectation and hope.

Mary: Teaching Us the Truth

Embracing the grace of a happy death is captured well by Robert Coles, the noted educator, who said, "Dying has more to do with living than death." Sister Mary Sax brought the truth of this grace home to me. A few weeks before she died in September of 2000, I asked her, "What is your truth, Mary?" She didn't need to respond because I already knew the answer. This was her truth: "Dying has more to do with living than death."

Mary taught this truth throughout her life but especially since December 20, 1999, when doctors confirmed the cancer growing in Mary's body. Sitting with Mary in her room that day, her eyes said to me, "You think this is about death? You think this is about fear? No, it's about life!" Mary showed me and many of her family, friends and community members how to live in the face of death. Mary taught us how to live without regret. Mary taught us the truth that "dying has more to do with living than death."

From the onset of her illness, she kept a cancer journal. Writing in her journal, Mary was both teacher and student. She filled the pages with memories of love, of the people she had met along the way, of the work that gave her life meaning, of the community in which she found her life's calling, of her family, whom she loved dearly. Her words in that journal reflect what I came to know in visiting with her the last few months: Mary was a woman of extraordinary faith who loved life. She taught those who knew her how to live life fully even in the face of death. Perhaps more than any person I have ever met, Mary was ready when the time came for her to die. She was ready for this primary moment of truth because she saw herself — and each person she knew and loved — as God's beloved. She lived her life as God's beloved and so loved life. This was her truth. This was the truth she lived.

Mary was the kind of woman religious communities love, because she was talented, hardworking, generous and gifted. In one sense, women like Mary who are both competent and compassionate become almost invisible in religious life. Most of the attention is paid to those who cause the wheel of community or ministry to squeak or to rattle or to roll off the road.

Ten days after she received the diagnosis of cancer, Mary wrote in her journal: "I'm too busy and generally feeling too well to realize the impact of what is happening." But confronting her disease, Mary wrote how "in many ways I have felt at peace and have tried to keep myself in God's hands. I am not afraid to die. If God is calling me home, I am ready, but I also want to live."

In teaching us the truth of her life, Mary also confronted her fears. In directly facing one of her fears ten days or so before she died, Mary did something that will have a lasting impact upon me. Her health had taken a dramatic turn for the worse, so Mary asked to celebrate the Sacrament of Anointing. Just before Mass, Mary said she would like to ask the sisters' forgiveness. Since it was the Jubilee year, she said, and we were focusing on forgiving debts both globally and personally, she wanted to ask the sisters in her community for their forgiveness.

Sitting in her wheelchair facing the community, she very graciously, courageously and humbly asked that if she had offended any sister in any way, whether they lived together years ago on mission or more recently while at the motherhouse, she begged their pardon. As Mary said that day, sometimes we hurt another's feelings without even knowing it. Sometimes we say things or fail to do something, and another is offended. So Mary asked for forgiveness.

What happened next is etched in my memory. The sisters came forward and offered Mary gestures of grace, blessing and prayer. It was a moving moment, and one that reflected the meaning of community as clearly as I have ever experienced it in religious life. A sister told me later that, of all people, Mary was the least likely to offend anyone. She was a gentle person. But Mary was simply doing what Mary did throughout her life. She was telling the truth, living the truth, following the truth, and teaching us the truth that had set her free.

In one woman's life, we see the themes reflected in this book — time, grace and sacred space — lived as an odyssey of faith. As her moment of truth drew near, Mary's room became a sacred space where she was surrounded by love. Her blood sisters and brothers, family, nieces and nephews and friends made many trips to see her. From California to New York, from coast to coast, her family converged on a small patch of promised land in southern Illinois to see her, to spend time with her and to be with her when she died. She was surrounded by the love of members of her community, good and faithful friends who were with her to the end. She was surrounded by the love of those with whom she served and ministered in so many places throughout the Midwest over the years.

Why was Mary surrounded by so much love? Because she was a woman "full of grace" who reflected the light of Christ. It was the light of Christ glowing and growing within her throughout her life that brought people together. Mary gathered those who were far off, brought them near, to a table where bread was broken and wine poured. She brought people to a light shining in the darkness, warming, beckoning and bringing others to the light of faith. Mary brought people to her deathbed where stories were told, songs sung and prayers said. And through it all Mary taught all of us to live what we profess to believe — that death is not the end but the beginning of a new life in Christ.

At the memorial Mass, Mary brought people together again to celebrate all the good graces God had bestowed upon her in this life and to celebrate her new life in Christ.

It's the truth: "Dying has more to do with living than death." It was the truth Mary lived and the moment of truth that ultimately set her free.

Prayer for the Grace of a Happy Death

The Hindu mystic Tagore wrote:
"The faith waiting in the heart of a seed
promises a miracle of life which it cannot prove at once."
His words affirm the message of Jesus:
"Unless a grain of wheat falls into the earth and dies,
it remains just a single grain;
but if it dies, it bears much fruit."

O God of Life,
when the time comes to journey from this world
to the one you have prepared for each of us,
open wide the door of your divine heart
and welcome me home.

May Saint Joseph, Patron of the Dying,
pray for my safe passage.
May Mary, Mother of Jesus,
pray for me, a sinner,
"now and at the hour of my death."

None of us knows the day or the hour,
so keep my heart ready, O God,
by remembering that "dying has more to do with life than death."
Help me make the most of each moment,
to taste and see, touch and smell, hear and tell
the truth.

This is my moment of truth:
that you, O God, chose to become one with us.
And though we were sinners,
your Son, Jesus Christ,
the Way, the Truth, and the Life,
showed us how to live
and how to die.

Following this Truth,
I commend my soul to you, O God,
now and at the hour of my death.
Amen.

Epilogue

The Day After: Finding Grace in the Ruins

Stop all the clocks, cut off the telephone,
Prevent the dog from barking with a juicy bone,
Silence the pianos and with muffled drum,
Bring out the coffin, let the mourners come.
—W.H. Auden

Look to my aching heart, speak to my empty heart,
You are the only one I cling to;
Where is your loving face, where is your saving grace,
Where is your mercy now?
—Marty Haugen

Certain events mark our time, our lives. Many in my parents' generation point to December 7, 1941, the "day that would live in infamy." Many in my generation will always remember where we were on November 22, 1963, the day President John F. Kennedy was assassinated. And now there is this date: September 11, 2001.

In his commentary the morning after Alex Chadwick said on National Public Radio that people in the United States woke up in "a different country." He was right: Now we live in a place where terrorists can board commercial airliners, hijack them and fly them into the World Trade Center and the Pentagon. President George W. Bush echoed this sentiment in his speech on September 20: "All of this was brought upon us in a single day, and night fell on a different world, a world where freedom itself is under attack."

September 11, 2001, brought people around the world to the most painful moment of truth imaginable. In that speech nine days after the terrorist attack, President Bush set a tone that resonated with many people not only in the United States but also throughout the world. It was a tone of comfort for those devastated by the attack and condemnation for those who perpetrated the terrorism. The president praised the spirit of courage and compassion on the part of those who in a time of crisis rise to the occasion and help those in need while also naming the cowardice and conceit of those whose concept of the truth is blinded by ideology. "We have seen their kind before," President Bush said. "They're the heirs of all the murderous ideologies of the twentieth century. By sacrificing human life to serve their radical visions, by abandoning every value except the will to power, they follow the path of fascism, Nazism and totalitarianism. And they will follow that path all the way to where it ends in history's unmarked grave of discarded lies."

When moments of truth like the terrible and tragic events of September 11 occur, we always remember precisely where we were when we heard the news. As W.H. Auden alludes, "all the clocks" stop. Time stands still and is forever etched on one's soul. I was in third grade that Friday afternoon in 1963 when Mrs. Ostrowski came back into the room after being called to the door by the principal. With tears in her eyes, she said, "The president has been shot in Dallas." Where were you on September 11 when you heard the news? I was standing on the sidewalk in front of the headquarters of my religious congregation in Liberty, Missouri. I was talking to Paul Aumen, a missionary in my community whom I had not seen in several years. I had a meeting at 9:00 when Annie Wilson, the assistant treasurer for my province, came running out of the building to tell us about a plane crashing into the World Trade Center. We turned on the television and watched as another plane hit the second tower. For the rest of the day, for the rest of that week, the television that for many has become the new altar in our domestic churches where we worship each night now became a true altar: a place where we gathered to pray, to listen for news.

But it was not good news. It was news that would change the world forever.

Listening to the news that day, I recall a commentator saying that "America is no longer a safe place." It is true that nothing like this — such a well-planned terrorist attack that targeted symbols of American democracy, defense and commerce — had ever happened before. But the world has not been a safe place for a very long time. We thought schools were safe places, and then came Columbine and so many other schools across the country where students turned guns on classmates and teachers. We thought synagogues were safe places, but then a man wielding a gun attacked children at a synagogue in Los Angeles.

New York City has never had the reputation as a "safe place." But when I visited there in September 1998 to give a retreat in midtown Manhattan, I felt safe as I walked the streets. On September 11, 2001, the attack was not from someone coming up from behind in an alley. This attack was from above, a plane carrying civilians who were on their way to the West Coast only to become victims in a suicide bomb attack on the World Trade Center as the plane loaded with fuel became a missile of mass destruction.

Some religious leaders, notably the Reverend Jerry Falwell, interpreted this attack from above as God's punishment on America for "having banished God from the public square and schools." Appearing on the *700 Club* with Pat Robertson, Falwell asserted that the terrorist attack was a doomsday scenario similar to Scripture's Sodom and Gomorrah. "I really believe that the pagans, and the abortionists, and the feminists, and the gays and the lesbians who are actively trying to make that an alternative lifestyle...I point the finger in their face and say, 'You helped this happen.'" He later apologized, but his harsh words were disgraceful — devoid of grace — precisely because they reflected the very attitudes of religious extremism that resulted in the terror and tragedy of September 11.

Watching the events unfold on television, I have rarely been as transfixed. Nothing else seemed to matter. Life changed in a profound way. The symbols of American commerce and capitalism crumbled, with thousands of people inside or on the ground killed by the falling debris. One of these was Father Mychal Judge, a Franciscan friar, who was chaplain for the New York City Fire Department. Father Mychal was hit by falling debris from the World Trade Center as he administered the Sacrament of the Anointing to a fallen firefighter. I met Father Mychal briefly a few years ago when I stayed at the St. Francis of Assisi Friary in midtown Manhattan where he lived and where I gave a day of recollection for religious in the area.

In the middle of absolute and utter chaos, Father Mychal, like his founder, St. Francis, was an instrument of peace and healing. At a worship service I attended following the terrorist attack, a favorite prayer of Father Mychal's was reprinted on the program:

> Lord, take me where You want me to go.
> Let me meet whom You want me to meet.
> Help me to say what You want me to say.
> And keep me from getting in Your way.

Father Mychal went into harm's way to bring healing and hope. When he was killed, the firefighters wrapped him in a white sheet and carried him to their firehouse across the street from the Friary in midtown Manhattan. They laid him in a bunk at the firehouse as the friars came over to pray.

So many stories. So much grief. So much anger. How do we find grace beneath the rubble of so much evil and death? How do we find that safe place within us and around us when we see the face of evil in the smoke that wrapped the World Trade Center? How do we respond to such atrocious and tragic moments of truth as the one that occurred on September 11, 2001?

The answers to these questions seemed elusive in the first few days and weeks following the terrorist attack. And yet we saw signs and heard stories where the grace of God came shining through our grief, our wounds, our anger and our fears. We heard the stories of "grace under fire" from relatives of the passengers on the flight that crashed in rural Pennsylvania who made the decision to overtake the hijackers. It was a moment of truth, a decision that would cost them their lives but undoubtedly saved so many others.

Grace was clearly evident in the stories of the firefighters, police officers and rescue workers who toiled around the clock and risked their own safety to reach those buried beneath the rubble at the Pentagon and the World Trade Center. We saw grace in the "hands-on" activity of compassion as thousands of people lined the streets to give the gift of life, their own precious blood, to victims in need. Grace enveloped the world in response to the terrorist attacks as people of all cultures, creeds and classes gathered in churches and synagogues, in mosques and pagodas, in parks and on street corners to pray for the victims and for peace. A spiritual energy was rekindled and released as people sought out loved ones, family and friends to pray and process, converse and console about the events that left many in the world hanging onto questions and holding on to one another.

Most of all, the events of September 11 reminded us all again how tenuous and fragile our lives are. As we have reflected often in these pages, moments of truth bring us to the precipice of decision about how we live our lives in a world that is passing away. Moments of truth provide us with opportunities to go deeper into the mystery of our relationship with God and with one another. Moments of truth encourage us to explore our own wounds, the scars we cannot hide that surface on our souls in the aftermath of events like those on September 11. In these moments of decision, we can allow the heat of our anger to melt the infrastructure of our very selves until we crumble under the weight of the evil inflicted upon us. Or we can direct that heat and turn it into a love that will transform the world.

In the wake of the terrorist attack, there were immediate calls for retaliation and revenge upon those who perpetrated this atrocity. In his speech on September 20, President Bush declared war on terrorism, saying it "will not end until every terrorist group of global reach has been found, stopped and defeated." But there were also calls for patience and perseverance. In that same speech, the president asked rhetorically, "What is expected of us?" And his answer: "I ask you to live your lives and hug your children." It seems so simple, yet it's so sacred and true. This is the safest place of all: in the shelter of another's arms.

In the aftermath of September 11, this is the sanctuary we seek. That phrase "a safe place" becomes flesh in the presence of those we love and those we trust. In this sacred space, we can allow our wounds

Defenseless under the night
Our world in stupor lies;
Yet, dotted everywhere,
Ironic points of light
Flash out wherever the Just
Exchange their messages:
May I, composed like them
Of Eros and of dust,
Beleaguered by the same
Negation and despair,
Show an affirming flame.